*Undomesticated*

# Undomesticated

INDY WEST

Archway Publishing books may be ordered through booksellers or by contacting:

Archway Publishing
1663 Liberty Drive
Bloomington, IN 47403
www.archwaypublishing.com
844-669-3957

Inspired by actual events

ISBN: 978-1-6657-0262-1 (sc)
ISBN: 978-1-6657-0263-8 (hc)
ISBN: 978-1-6657-0264-5 (e)

Library of Congress Control Number: 2021902121

Print information available on the last page.

Archway Publishing rev. date: 8/2/2021

*This book is dedicated to* my four children. May you always listen to the depth of your essence and create a fulfilling, individual path of self-evolution inclusive of love, honor, respect, and, most of all, truth. Live with authentic passion and by your wild and untamed hearts.

To the men in my heart, you all have, in the most beautiful and potently genuine ways, helped my soul grow and have elevated my life. You know you have a part of my heart that will only belong to you. I will love you each with all that I am for eternity.

Domesticated: verb

To convert to domestic uses, tame
To accustom to household life
To make more ordinary, familiar, acceptable

Tame, ordinary, convert …

*Fuck this.*

# Invictus

Out of the night that covers me,
Black as the Pit from pole to pole,
I thank whatever gods may be
For my unconquerable soul.

In the fell clutch of circumstance
I have not winced nor cried aloud.
Under the bludgeonings of chance
My head is bloody, but unbowed.

Beyond this place of wrath and tears
Looms but the Horror of the shade,
And yet the menace of the years
Finds, and shall find, me unafraid.

It matters not how strait the gate,
How charged with punishments the scroll,
I am the master of my fate:
I am the captain of my soul.

—William Earnest Henley,
English poet, 1849–1903

# INTRODUCTION

To be what I would consider a "free spirit" has much difficulty and acceptance in a world where most people feel the intense need to follow with the flow and ease of a conformed society. I do not follow into conformity. Nor do I consider myself a leader. I just want to *be*. I want to explore with unblocked curiosity, to discover the vast complexities of my own self so that I can understand and gain wisdom to propel myself forward on my journey here and ever after.

I am forty-four years old. Some might say that I am in a crisis, midlife. Some call it the transition period, some will call it crazy, and some will say I'm blindsided, in a fog, going through menopause, or whatever they like, but it makes no difference to me. As Dr. Seuss's delicate yet powerful wisdom has long been engrained in my head, "Be who you are and say what you feel, because those that mind don't matter and those that matter don't mind" (Theodor Seuss Geisel, 1904–1991). Whatever this is, it is changing me. It is challenging me. It is charging me. I like it and invite it because without change is stagnation, and then, with stagnation, you wilt and rot. How grossly unbecoming. Someone once said, "The land of familiarity belongs to the dead." That disgusted me. I want to grow and be in the light, to live unbridled and to love, without boundary, every breathing moment. I want to live life against the grain, the road less traveled, all of it, so that I do not fall into routine (into that societal flow that utterly bores me). I do not want to be normal and ordinary. I want to be abnormal in a wild yet poetic way and live an extraordinary life. I will not be categorized. I will not join one-minded membership groups. I am not egocentric by any means. I just want to explore and keep exploring. The idea of numbing personal contemplation by means of integrating the self into a common thought group or membership of well-regulated structure fucks with me. To me, it declares, "Think only like us," "be exactly like us," "behave like us," and that strips away the very voice I want pronounced and outspoken with individualized acuity. I need this voice to speak and seek/contemplate/dream. I need it to proclaim independence so I can independently evolve. I am *never* done.

My grandfather once told me, "Nothing is too sacred to be questioned, and that truth is strong enough to withstand challenge." I have held that in my heart from the day he said it. It resonates with me on levels I've yet to comprehend. I "muse in" and explore the details of depth in almost everything. Sometimes, I find pleasure in outspoken discourse/debate, and other times I am still and listen, ponder, saturate, and explore personal meaning, adopting what I need, then discarding the crap I feel is useless to my endeavors.

Regardless, I long for magnitude on a daily basis. To me, deep insight and the vastness of wonder are tools utilized for expansion of self. Surface is mundane to me, causing anguish in my mind and in my soul. It is colorless. It is devitalizing. If there is no more than an outer shell, I'm simply uninterested. I don't want to overthink things, and I avoid the analysis/paralysis type of pondering, yet sometimes I do. I think being a seeker of truth and wanting to love with all my capacity and live with exultant happiness can be challenging—lonely, as well as, exhausting. However, the expectation in what I deem as a necessary life, a purposeful and meaningful life, is to avail life itself through lessons and the knowledge gained in those lessons and to be able to move forward with collective wisdom and an unbreakable spirit to soar to higher realms in this life and the ever after. This is me.

Several years back I began my zeal for writing as an outlet of emotion and as an inlet of communication with myself. Life started to face drastic changes. I felt drawn to my pen, as it felt safe and secure to divulge the inside of me to something I could trust without any compromise. So with pen in my hand, I started writing incessantly. Often, I felt as if the pen were magical, as if someone came through me, wrote for me, wrote to me. I couldn't wait some nights to secure a secret place and whisper my soul to the pages that effortlessly took form into my story. My transcendence from challenging chaos and steel armor resistance then surrendering to the uncertainty and finally accepting the unrelenting drive to charge into change has been as tempestuous as it has been tranquil.

What's this story about anyway? I guess it's about a journey. My journey. A quest of self-discovery at that moment in our lives that pulls and pushes us to become so much more. Within the ridiculous chaos lies the secret seed of promise and transcendence of becoming more than subservience to the status quo. More than just being convinced a stage will pass if you simply look the other way. The drive, which lies deep inside that is ready to launch at the most precise moment in time, has specific and personal agendas. Drive that I could not suppress the day it was ready to lift off.

# PART 1

## Falling Out

You are not the victim of the world, but rather the master of your own destiny. It is your choices and decisions that determine your destiny.

—Roy T. Bennett

*My long yet beautiful and* rewarding young mothering phase had slowed down as my children were approaching ages of an earned youthful independence. I began to look forward to a couple of hours each day to myself with less of a watchful eye on them and give permission for their personal advancement. I still was dedicated to taking care of my children, husband, and the home. I just didn't need it to consume all my minutes. However, I had found that these little, scattered fragments of the day were not sufficient to figure out much of anything. The only way to allow myself a broader perspective was to gently pull away from the circle just a little more so I could look around me with a perspective I had not seen before. A view from the perimeter to perhaps seek an understanding of where I wanted to take myself in the next life chapter or even some kind of understanding of the reason I felt compelled to search for more.

Sitting on the outside for some time had allowed me to be pensive about myself and my family life. The good and the bad, the acceptable and unacceptable. I thought about the kind of wife I had been. Was he happy with me? Satisfied with me? Did he feel my dedication to him, our marriage, and our children? Did he notice at all? I thought about how deeply I loved him, almost too much. I may have been blinded by what I was questioning now as unacceptable. Was I just going through the motions and unable to see this before?

I had to make this necessary change of sitting on the outside for my life to continue with movement. Not just going through those motions but for it to evolve and to live my moments in that exultation I so craved. Every day I was alive, I wanted to experience this exultation. As that creeping of dissatisfaction took course through me, it began shadowing the clarity of purpose I once knew from my domesticated life as a housewife.

A domesticated housewife, ugh, that felt like a disguise over who I was underneath it all. A disguise that could slowly suffocate me. I needed to move away from feeling like this, whatever the consequences. I suddenly wanted and needed nothing else but being in the driver's seat with my own map and compass, with bold direction and without wearing a floral apron.

Great comfort was developing in this place I created by being on the perimeter. I could still be supportive and attentive to my husband's needs, and I could still function as if nothing had changed as a mother. He was busy and consumed with work most often anyway, while I was full throttle with my blue-sky world of discovery. It sustained me for a long duration—four extensive years—until recently, when the strong demand from my husband to come back into that domesticated world pushed me even further out into the call of the mysterious wild.

I felt free out there, even if the freedom was counterfeit or borrowed or just my own fleeting perception. I also no longer wanted to accept anyone demanding me to do anything. So I continued on with uninterrupted vengeance. What unintentionally and, most unfortunately, transpired through my sidesteps, coupled with my husband's extreme preoccupation with his business, is that the intimate part of the us in our marriage declined, then significantly derailed. I could still have crazy, amazing sex, but that deep closeness and connection that stirred my soul was gone for me, and I began to feel disgustingly numb.

I can recall countless moments of raw and exciting sex, yet I was removed and disengaged from him. It was so foreign from the way I used to let myself go into him—as if we were one soul, two bodies, as we used to describe. I coaxed myself to pretend to connect, but he eventually took notice. I could feel and see the fear, annoyance, and suspicion birthing in his eyes as our once felt unity was slipping away. It anguished me that this was happening, but it was. It was then that he started to really pay attention, yet the attention was not out of benevolent concern. It was out of selfish command. He tried and tried and continues to try to knock on the door of my heart. I am no longer there.

I wrote feverishly in my journal.

Fantasy creeped into my days to escape. I looked back on my life and thought about how good I had always been. I was proud of my integrity and of the character I had built and sustained. Perhaps it was the reason I was typically unabashed in my days with contentment in ethical quality. Yet a part of me had emerged from somewhere alien to me that wanted to tiptoe up to the no crossing line, and maybe rebel against the good and feel what it would be like to be a little audacious. I did not want to hurt anyone, and I knew that I was solely thinking of myself here and I did not mean to sound selfish. However, with incessant years of selfless devotion to this uninterrupted good, perhaps I was seduced by defiance. I wanted to yield to it when this something inside of me would not let up.

This is only a fantasy in my own world and perhaps it really isn't a bad thing at all. I could just be in a state of intoxicating desire to become more—to experience more. This is all me. I take full responsibility for my thoughts, dreams, desires, and actions.

I am the master of my fate, the captain of my soul.

—William Earnest Henley

This ignites a fire inside of me just writing and thinking about it. The more confident I am about flaming the fire of desire, the more turned on and driven I become.

A lot of people I know are satisfied with mainstream. They enjoy the comfort and safety of daily ritual, the knowing and planning of their lives in full, organized mechanical structure. It's good for some people, it's good for many people, and that's okay for them. It is not so good for me, and I don't like the word OK. Not anymore. I wake in the morning and feel life's surging invite. It teases me with adventure and makes my senses come alive with spontaneity and want. I crave the day, and if I can't get to the good stuff and the day slips away from me without the play together, I get very restless. I feel let down, as if I let life itself down.

In a way, I feel I owe life all I have of myself, and I want to embrace its supposed or imagined request of me. I don't mean this in a way where I am not working in a job or career and I just go off and do whatever I want. I mean it in the inward sense of life's prosperous joy waiting to be embodied within us, and hear life itself through our laughter outward, feel itself when we take a moment to touch nature, see itself as reflection as we deeply stare into the eyes of another soul. This is how we should give back to it. I desperately want to give back to it. I want to feel its pulse of vitality through every facet of my existence. My minuscule entity on this vast planet absorbing the vivacity of life—it is just so powerful. How could anyone just settle into a linear life? Such an insult to existence. I laugh as I write because this is classic "midlife" banter ... but, *why*? *Why* do we feel it? Fuck it. I love it. I absolutely am *in love* with it. It is movement. Movement is the vessel to inspiration.

I witness a frazzled mother with her child in the store sometimes, wrestling with her emotions, wrestling with her overload. I adored every minute of this when I was engaged within it. But now I want nothing to do with new babies and heavily dependent husbands. I think with all the hyper-focused energy I spent exclusively on marriage and mothering, it has somewhat left a part of me unfulfilled. Did I neglect my own self? I loved giving to people I loved and cared for, and still do. But I guess I just want to give a little in my direction, just for this moment, and play out these longings begging me to pay attention to.

Pay attention! Longings for adventure, longings for passion, longings for excitement, and action, and the mortality of boredom. I think often that we attempt to pacify our souls in keeping ourselves distracted within our jobs or responsibilities. Yet our souls were meant to always feel the surge to run wild in seeking and discovering our dreams, and then the embodying of "personal truth." With so much heavy expectation on how you *should* be, *ought to be*, supposed to be, I think I may have slipped into a semblance of comfort and familiarity, but it is no longer comforting. It is caving. Now, I am clawing out. I crave to run, I crave the mystery, I crave the barbaric wild, and I do not think I can stop its hailing command.

I am falling out of my constraints, my constants. I am falling away from what I am accustomed to. I fear it and I tremble. I crave it and I excite.

> There are not mistakes. The events we bring upon ourselves, no matter how unpleasant, are necessary in order to learn what we need to learn; whatever step we take, they're necessary to reach the places we've chosen to go.
>
> —Richard Bach

## *Journal*
August 2011

I don't know the precise moment I shifted inside. There is subtle but noticeable movement within as I am becoming altered. The strange part is I am not at all fearful of said movement, which has provoked my attention to revise my own self. In fact, I welcome it. I am ready to experience the life lessons I know that are lying ahead of me. I have some complicated obstacles though. It is going to be tough. Well, at least it seems tough when you are looking in from the sideline. It may become quite easy when I am faced with the actuality and realness of the moment.

I haven't many regrets in my forty-three years of life. I think the decisions I have made have been good ones. Solid, from integrity and decent moral conduct. Perhaps it is why I am happy. Am I happy? Really?

I love what Ralph Waldo Emerson said in his writings.

The good are befriended even by weakness and defect. As no man ever had a point of pride that was not injurious to him, so no man had ever a defect that was not somewhere made useful to him. Has he a defect of temper that unfits him to live in society? Thereby he is driven to entertain himself alone, and acquire habits of self-help; and thus, like the wounded oyster, he mends his shell with pearl. Our strength grows out of our weakness. The indignation which arms itself with secret forces does not awaken until we are pricked and stung and sorely assailed. A great man is always willing to be little. Whilst he sits on the cushion of advantages, he goes to sleep. When he is pushed, tormented, defeated, he has a chance to learn something: he has been put on his wits, on his manhood; he has gained facts; learns his ignorance; is cured of the insanity of conceit, has got moderation and real skill.

Wow—a chance to *learn* something.

*Journal*
August 2011

In the past, my husband was an amazing person to whom I have given my heart. It has not been all easy, of course, but I am learning along the way, as I am sure he has. I have always been a very faithful wife to him, never, ever desiring any other man at all. He has been "king" for the twenty-five years we have been together. I have dreamt of sitting on a front porch swing, watching the physical sunset in the winter of our existence with him as well as our "life's sunset" and all we accomplished together as a couple. I love the solidity and perfection of it all. Its purity, its beauty, its romance. But is it? Just who's reality is that, anyway? Reality is far different from my dream.

He really hasn't been as faithful to me, with the incessant obsession of looking/lusting at other women all throughout our relationship. I really don't think he has ever slept with another woman, but in all honesty, I couldn't say for sure. I lost trust in our relationship long ago due to these outward desires, his ongoing lying with many other different issues, and disrespectful decisions with our financial future that obligated me/us to enormous, catastrophic debt. Consequently, there has been an upheaval of a massive accumulation of disrespect, and over the years, it's been tough to accept and live with. I thought that the love I have would/could endure everything, including the significant lack of respect. I had such a fairytale expectation of what a relationship was and could be, and I think I finally just gave it up somewhere along the way. I was let down. Perhaps I was in love with the idea of him/us, the fairytale, the dream. I let myself down.

> When you find your path, you must not be afraid. You need to have sufficient courage to make mistakes. Disappointment, defeat, and despair are the tools God uses to show us the way.
> —Paulo Coelho, Brida

Looking back on it, this was the start of noticing that there was something inside myself that was clearly unfulfilled. I missed that part of me that was my own and that was solid, and I longed to bring her back out. Little did I know, I had missed a lot, and I was not about to flirt with getting to know myself again. I was about to let everything pour out, cleanse myself, pull in resilience, and come back at full force. I had been tucked away too long. Now, I just want to engage within myself, fully awake and to feel the me resurface and come alive. My soul started to rebel against my old habits, and I started paying more attention to the mystery of the spirit and the pulls of the universe and how my soul danced around my enticing new thought processes that were coming at me from all different directions, tantalizing me and lifting me with that one word that charged me with anticipation and excitement. The word *possibility.*

Don't be afraid to be confused. Try to remain
permanently confused. Anything is possible.
Stay open, forever, so open it hurts, and then
open up some more, until the day you die,
world without end.

—George Saunders

*Journal*
August 2011

Daydreams and fantasy are normal for everyone, including
sexual fantasy. In my sexual fantasies, he has no name, no
face, but he masters arousal. I have been fantasizing a lot. I
imagine him shoving me against an old alley wall on a hot,
sultry summer night in an abrupt and intense moment of lust,
passion, unrelenting want, chemistry, and desire. I want to
be taken completely. His mouth on mine, then his imperious
tongue exploring and tasting all of me. Grabbing me and
claiming me adamantly, moving and pressing on me so that
I can feel his virility. Harassing me with the avidity of what
will never be. Breathing rapidly with growling low moans of
temporary surrender that are saturating through our undeni-
able connection. Hearts pounding, erotic, potent, completely
lost in one brief and unforgettable moment.

Fucking incredible. I can feel it now as if it actually happened. I wonder what I would do in a situation like that in
real life. How would I respond? Would I refuse and reject
out of commitment as well as strong personal values? Would
I succumb and surrender in the moment of command and
connection?

Two different worlds, one delirious and illusory and the
other altruistic and logical. I need fantasy to take me places

for an escape. Maybe it is the boredom, maybe a little unsatisfied. Just very much in need of overwhelming, voracious passion that makes my blood boil with mind-blowing, disruptive highs. I like the details I can put into this realm without holding back. I "go away" there, and I am without boundary. I am unattached to anyone or anything. I make anything possible. I attempt to exchange these fantasies with daring and crazy escapades in my conscious world. I have a bucket list of adventures that I will complete. Perhaps it will temporarily pacify the rabidity of sexual want that disturbs me in these extreme fantasies. I beg for the savage adventure to supersede the lure of dangerous fantasy. Every day, I beg my God to keep me sound and stable.

Running is my deliverance into my fantasy world, so I go running almost every day and use this time to play my music that is highly sexual, dirty, hard—explicit rock or heavy metal. I can't wait to sweat to it. I can't wait to drive myself into my realm of this world where I treat myself to strength, power, will, determination, motivation, and getting out of it what I put into it. I like working hard at something and envisioning its deserved, inevitable, and timely outcome of accomplishment. I have now pushed myself hard into adventure because it's the closest thing to choke all creeping of boredom. I fucking hate to be bored. It's so flat and dormant. So obliterating. I need to keep moving in some way that is physical and in all ways mental. It fuels my being and ignites my soul. It grounds me in discipline and unites me with my path (whatever the fuck that may be). It just feels right so I am going to continue to do it for as long as my body will allow it.

> Fantasy is hardly an escape from reality. It is
> a way of understanding it.
> —Lloyd Alexander

We have circumstances that we are faced with every day. We make choices from those circumstances. Sometimes choices feel in aligned perfection, but sometimes, we are completely wondering why in the hell we made a certain choice when it is uncomfortable or appears to be wrong. But to me, there are *no* wrong choices and no coincidences. *Experience it!* Don't fight it. Perhaps choice is a gateway for unleashing our restrictions in order to grow and to fulfill every possibility of our existence. This stirs me. Fear is blanketed. Boredom is temporarily nullified. I'm electrified with enthusiasm as it detoxifies the darkness and fills it with a purity that replaces void with illumination. I am in movement like the undying ocean.

> Either you decide to stay in the shallow end of the pool, or you go out in the ocean.
> —Christopher Reeves

> The least movement is of importance to all nature. The entire ocean is affected by a pebble.
> —Blaise Pascal

Am I creating a self-fulfilled prophecy? Am I giving myself permission to move forward with what has chiseled an opening of momentum? A challenging and uncertain pursuit of chance, of hope, of a dream of near unwavering trust I have convinced myself of and the wholeness that will surely accompany the outcome if I just simply persist? Am I responsible for the consequences that follow or are consequences a mere reflection of cause and effect, of the natural flow of the cosmos? I study my words past written, and although they are strongly felt with urgency, what if I have only persuaded myself to proceed with self-growth by claiming an almost divine associated action out of casual human lethargy during midlife "crisis"? Am I just another story? I want more depth than a whimsical novel. I want to fully embrace the quantum level of all dimensions of existence and to trust in individual significance, gifts to relinquish as well as receive from this world, and a legend that will forever live on.

August 2011

I have escaped my own home. I have very little patience right now in my life. Don't know why. I suppose the chaos, the bickering, the moods, the mess. I can't find solitude, and I can't feel me at all. I feel buried. I will have to work on this, for sure, because I can't really run away every time I become stifled. I can't feel me. Jesus. How lame is that. I should be me, feel me completely, through and through, under any circumstance, no matter what. Amen. I run though. I run as fast as I can.

I once heard a local lecturer voice this profound statement: "We cannot deny fear. There is darkness out there and we cannot turn away from it. What we can do is stand in the light and once there, we look through fear."

Is it fear that I am running from? Fear of what I am to become every time I walk in the doors to the expected domestication of household life? I walk through the doors anyway, and I turn away from my thoughts, and I smile at my beautiful children. They are of serene comfort to me. Of utmost reward. I look at my husband, and I force a smile as my insides grip with tension. Is this why, I fear? Is he the reason I flee?

Changing.

I look at myself as an observer from the outside and notice things that I do not yet understand, but something deeper within me, quite confidently does. I am doing things on a daily basis that are strange, but I am compelled to do them anyway. I remember when I was pregnant with my first baby and I would prepare for my child by mere instinct alone. I had never had a baby, so how was I supposed to know what to expect aside from books and elder example? Instinct took over when the baby arrived, and I proceeded in my most natural state. I recognize the parallel. Instinct, deeply rooted, inborn, is preparing me, yet this time I have no idea what the fuck I am preparing for. Change is both rousing and daunting. This knowing inside anticipates the upcoming adventure of newness and of an unidentified thrill and this knowing inside is also warning of extreme discomfort and uncertainty. I grieve for an unspecified loss that I have yet to abandon, that is familiar, and at one time I must have cherished, as the grieving, I sense, will be excruciating.

Is it my marriage? Do I want to admit to myself that this could be at its end? Marriage is the foundation of my family, yet it is now weak and unstable. I have contributed to its frailty, and if I am convinced of its detriment, ultimately, I will be responsible for the demise of it. I am the one falling out, yet past actions have consequences that can no longer be concealed. My heart aches with void rather than fulfilment, and I believe that once the heart has reached a place that crosses into another domain, salvation has been defeated. I know I will have to make a decision on something that I have been accustomed to versus something that is new. I believe my heart will ultimately guide me. *If* It's my marriage, I'm not sure I even have control of retaining love. It is written in some "save your marriage" books that we can reconnect or reestablish love should it become delicate by any kind of threat. I have tried this many times, for multiple years, in many different forms, but my ego is either too stubborn, my attempts too meager, or my heart within my soul has crossed into that unspoken territory and I have no control of it returning no matter how hard I push my human endeavors and attempt to fuse a knowing heart to an unknowing mind. We have no supremacy in mind over the authority of heart; nor do we have control with whom we fall in love with or stay in love with. Love is dominant, and when it awakens in validity, we must oblige. It is the law of love—powerful, pinnacle, beautiful, unmistakable—and when love leaves us, we will heavily grieve but we must release, give thanks and let it go. It is the law of honor.

> All great changes are preceded by chaos.
> —Deepak Chopra

*Journal*
Late December 2011

I sense a very chaotic year. I will be challenged by many things, but I am ready. I was so numb during the holidays in December. It was coldly depressing and disturbing. I was happy to take down the decorations and store them away. I longed for spring. I longed for renewal. I longed for better times, different and new times. Often, I think something is very wrong with me. I look at my suitable home, my happy children who are thankfully oblivious with my everyday mind- fuck of utter confusion and an unrelenting urge to uncover the mystery of this pull to new directions. My husband is disrupted greatly by my fall to the outside of "us" and my pursuit in seeking personal meaning. He is not where I am. He knows the past four years had damaging repercussions to our marriage, yet he is convinced it will work out and simply continue on. Had this been said to me just two years ago, when I begged and pleaded with him to go to marriage counseling, it would have sounded enticing to me. Now I am unmoved and have let go of that appeal and charm, as it no longer seems to coax emotion. I feel hardened up inside. My typical sensitive side should conjure up an expression of sadness from the collapse or loss of something so meaningful, yet I do not feel that at all. Perhaps, I have not faced the reality of this, and I linger in purgatory states of the relationship, almost as if I am on standby. It is fucked up. Does God or whoever/whatever have a plan for me? Do we want a higher power to be responsible so we don't bear all the painful accountability? I try to control personal circumstances, yet the harder I push and try to gain mastery, the more uptight, uncomfortable, and powerless I actually become. Is my surrender the answer for clarity? Maybe we can put the thought out there and nurture it with intention, but not command the outcome? Release and detach without a confirmed conclusion. Is this the throttle for victory? Trust?

I want to be courageous in my attempts to trial my thoughts in practice instead of theory. Theory gets you nowhere. Mere theory is for the weak. Results come after the rehearsal and habit, in the trial and error, in the personal discovery of a way of life that becomes fulfilling for that individual. I can't succumb to "good enough," because it is not. Strategies may change innumerable times before the grand design is even implemented. Trial and error. I will be tenacious in this pursuit of my truth, and peace will avail upon my surrender when the time is right to concede in unity with universal call, universal plan, and universal conclusion—or whatever bullshit force I need as a companion with my said venture. Here I go.

> The greatness of the man's power is the measure of his surrender.
>
> —William Booth

> If you live in the light, you will keep an open mind and your faith will not be threatened by new discoveries and insights. Valor consists in self recovery … In the service of Truth, you

must be willing to endure the scorn of those
little minds that cherish a foolish consistency.
If you would be a man, speak today in words
as hard as cannonballs, and tomorrow speak
what tomorrow thinks in hard words again,
though it contradict everything you said
today.

　　　　　　　　　　　　　—Ralph Waldo Emerson

My husband's ongoing attacks of belittling and harshly shaming remarks regarding my new changing energy has been painful to say the least, but they also started depleting any enthusiasm at wanting to hang around him at all. He seems to not much care, for this woman that is emerging. I can't shut down, won't. I was listening to Tony Robbins, an internationally recognized speaker, and his talk on polarity. It is just so fascinating to me. Through some of the ideas in his lecture, I felt like I was grasping some confirmation or validation of what could have happened in our relationship the past three years. It just became so obvious to me through Tony's viewpoints, which seemed to match issues with ours. I guess I should not have shared this with my husband, but I was so excited to have had a breakthrough of plausible ideas so that mending could have a possible renewal. When we started having trouble, I voiced how I could help, and I did, and he was appreciative. I talked about some ways he could help, but he didn't. Either having no time, being uninterested, or whatever the reason, he put more and more effort into his business and absolutely nothing into us. I felt he rejected the marriage and that he deemed it inconsequential, and I became increasingly let down, lonely, and ultimately resentful. Now, as things seem to barely hang on and I have changed to this slightly callous, unemotional, hard person while driving my energy into self-focus, obviously he has a big problem with me.

He wants me back the way I was, the good little housewife. Quiet, obedient to the house and children and of course to him. It might take some time for me to unravel a bit. Lick my wounds in private and venture back at it. Maybe I will build upon the emotional scars that are developing and something explosive will come about in a great course of personal push and enterprise. It is the push through the obstacle that is challenging, but victory awaits those that endure then conquer the threatening strain. Time is constant movement; I am not sitting still.

> Resentment seems to have been given to us by nature for a defense, and for a defense only. It is the safeguard of justice and the security of innocence.
>
> —Adam Smith

> Consciousness is only possible through change: change is only possible through movement.
>
> —Aldous Huxley

*Journal*
December 12, 2011

I am in such a funk. I am trying to do everything I can not to be spiritless, but I am still experiencing debilitating, fucking dullness. I want some fun and excitement, some mind stimulation that makes me challenge my own belief system. I feel life is maintaining flatness, reminds me of my home state in the deep farmlands of the Midwest. Looking out over those flat-ass corn and soybean fields—fuck, man. The only one that can fix this is me. I know this. I like working my body hard, but I need other things. Deeper, philosophical, spiritual conversations with people that perplex me and mystify me, that cause my mouth to drop open with *thought*. God, I need help. This is, again, so cliché of a midlife crisis. Maybe having a midlife crisis opens us to an evaluation that is pertinent to the construction of wholeness. Perhaps midlife is that brutal climb to the precipice to reach transcendental awareness/opportunity. Perhaps it is the rite of passage to purpose and light and wisdom. Perhaps I am claiming midlife to be this grand avenue when I am just utterly ridiculous and fucked up with zero direction and zero sense down a dead end. What the fuck am I going to do with all this? This fucking midlife disorientation. It seems like I am trapped in my own self-imposed cave. I have all my responsibilities with the kids and my husband and this house. I work out, eat, shower and run a couple of errands, and then suddenly, kids come home. Then homework, dinner, cleanup, bedtime routines. Hours are utilized at increasingly rapid speeds, but it is aimlessly exhausting. I feel like I never accomplish anything of importance or relevance, and I know that I have something greater inside to contribute. I don't need to change the world or have my face plastered on an iconic magazine or on a breakfast cereal box, but I feel something, something great inside. I was meant to do something great. I feel muted, and I want to rise ferociously. Are you there, God? Please tell me what to do. Guide me, lead me, teach me. What is this? Funny how we all reach out to "God" in a crisis. I didn't do that when all was copacetic. How stupid. How disloyal I am if there even is a God.

*Journal*
January 10, 2012

I fill up partially with a sliver of hope, and it drains from me faster than I can claim it. Emptiness looms. I feel I have become unhappy now most of my days although I still get great satisfaction out of a sunrise, my workouts, the sunset, and most of all, my children's smiles and their beautiful innocence. There are things about my husband that are so unusual and have now become frightening to me, peculiar behavior that perhaps I am beginning to take notice of, or perhaps it has always been present, but I chose to be impervious. This current awareness makes it seem as if he takes from me. Robs me of self. My entire soul evacuates, and I am left with just a confused brain and a vacuous body because draining situations become over consuming and I become progressively elusive. What am I going to do? I have a very hard time faking marital happiness to myself and around my kids. I have a hard time with faking anything. What will I do to change all this?

April 23, 2012

I love sex. I love sex with my husband as the impending reality drifts away momentarily. Sex is often our only connection as it has always been outstanding physically from day one together. Friday nights and Saturdays are typical days to escape into this physical connection with him, and I shut out the heaviness and attempt to fall into what we had. As Sunday rolls in, I could tell he was spiraling down and becoming dismal, cold, and eerie again. I kept my distance, but then he was really angry with me for not listening to his opinion about the dog. The fucking dog? I tried so hard to just be in my pseudo-happy bubble and focus on matters of greater importance, but his increasingly dark energy is strong and overwhelming at times. When I cannot escape, I try to envision a steel case around myself, but his intrusion is unrelenting, and I break and succumb to whatever I need to do to appease him. Monday, he left for Toronto on business, but he was still in the mood even with the physical distance between us. After days of this, I begin to feel very angry and resentful toward him for treating me spitefully. I am offended because of all that I put up with currently and in our past with his lies and deceit with his pornography addiction that still, after many years of that degrading, insulting bullshit, still goes on, and then, dealing with the loans he secretly took out and the immense and continued out-of-control spending and debt. Promises and talk about our secure financial future have all become heresy to me now, and I have assumed a weird acceptance of his lying and have adopted an "oh, well" attitude to his appeal to porn and vulgar desires toward very young women within the pornography. I am accustomed to his many job losses and/or job changes, accepting his position of victimhood of "too hard, too much, too this or too that." I believed him and the story that accompanied him. I wanted to support him and wanted to stand by everything with him. When there is a disagreement and I state my testimonies, he attacks with forceful persuasion until he captures my "side" and shames it to devastation. Even the small things—even when I don't want to listen to him about a dog-grooming appointment? *What the fuck?* I feel very disrespected, cheated, underestimated, and taken for granted. I don't want to be here. I want to run away, but I have nowhere to go, and I will *never* leave without my children. I need to protect them and care for them. I love them so much. They *are* my world. I feel engulfed in the viscosity of thick *fuck*. I am struggling to hold onto my spirit and happiness, and I do not want to bail out of my marriage like a pussy, but I feel like there is nothing here but chaos and struggle and suffocation of spirit. So I retreat, and I lose myself in the daydreams and escape back into beautiful fantasy where there is an outlet of a spark. Get my head on here. I have to be a good mother. I have to be a good mother. I have nothing else. I must press on and through this. I must press on. I must. *Fuck*, I am so tired.

When I drift off in a craving, I think how essential it is for me to experience being loved, passionately, romantically, and deeply again. I need somebody who will love me and connect with the goodness that I know I am. To see and respect all of me. I am so sick of walking on eggshells. I am sick of being forced to believe through incredible, talented manipulation that I am so wrong all the time for being vocal with my outward testimony, especially of the inner hurt I attempt to express to him. Maybe I just need some simple validation of understanding these genuine feelings. I'm sick of being a punching bag. I am sick of the same weekends of the same shit and the same lowball moods. I get nervous that my husband is coming home from work and I have to deal with his predictable yet intimidating and threatening states of mind and that I am blamed for whatever disconcerting mood he uncloaks in. I really just want to love and be loved. I need love. It is a requisite of my existence. I'm extremely vulnerable right now. I don't like feeling like this. I'm not sure what will emerge from closeting this desperation for love, too long. I'm vulnerable, and that is really not a good thing, or is it? I want to remain strong and keep my head from spinning atop a weary, critical heart. I need something in me to keep my integrity grounded. However, sometimes, most times, I want to rebel against it all.

I keep running into specific people all the time, and it makes me wonder if I am inviting these people into my life? Is it all coincidence, or are there no coincidences? Why is it that I will be thinking of someone in particular and then they show up? Often times, I try to ignore the idea of fate, and then they almost instantaneously pop in when I try to deny fate's trial on my conscience. Are there reasons for these people to pull them into my world for experiences, or am I just creating something out of nothing? Am I desperate? I question and ponder everything. It's exhausting. It's enticing.

> There are no coincidences.  The soul seeks its own path
> —Angela Gwinner

*Journal*
June 9, 2012

I feel incredibly stuck. I wish I had money so I could leave here and figure my life out with just myself and my children. How can I, though? Me getting out of this seems impossible, and I disgust myself by the frailty of mentioning the word "impossible." I'm so torn. *Fuck.* I need to imitate happiness and contentment for my children. They need stability. They need me for strength and structure and security. I am the example here. Can I do this for another ten years? Oh my God, I will be fifty-four years old and nothing gained in personal achievement and nothing saved financially while I quarantine my spirit. I feel glued to this scenario. I have to go inward while I am with everyone and find greater sources of empowerment. Be silent and still (well, somewhat still anyway). God, help me, please, please. I am now at the point of begging.

> The only difference between a rut and a grave are the dimensions.
> —Ellen Glasgow

Don't wait for the right answer and the golden path to present themselves. This is precisely why you're stuck. Starting without seeing the end is difficult, so we often wait until we see the end, scanning relentlessly for the right way, the best way and the perfect way. The way to get unstuck is to start down the wrong path, right now. As you start moving you can't help but improve, can't help but incrementally find yourself getting back to your North star.

—Seth Godin

I saw a psychic today with my sister while visiting her in the Great Lakes area. I wonder if the cards are just a random shuffle, coupled with a clever story to come close within a conjecture of some sucker's need for life guidance. Or does ghost/spirit-like energy indeed tell the secrets so she can then relay that information with veracity? Seemingly accurate accounts on my reading, though, and it's hard to deny her authenticity. I may still be skeptical and may debate the proposed outcome as something that could indeed wrap around any Jane Doe's life. "An attraction to another that is married that will lead into a magical love affair?" A husband who "can't be felt," who is "absent … not here." "A feeling of "being trapped" and "a strong need for a change that will present itself over and over again until I take notice," "a soul that is restless" "that magical love that can't be denied as we cannot be separated." Hmmmmm, dead-on accurate except the magical love affair. WTF? Probably my incessant fantasy that persists on a daily basis. That energy must be exceedingly prominent because she kept going back to that one card, smiling and shaking her head. She said, "My angel is telling me to really pay attention to this because this man is very, very important in your life as

well as your importance in his life." Very intriguing, frightening, strange, and exquisite. I love the mystical.

   After what the psychic said, will I be looking for situations
to identify with her information? I am so attracted to the mystical, but I become skeptical when logic grips my intellect. I know
we are capable of creating extensions to a story from a story, but
can I dismiss the possible impression or design of something
greater that I have no control over? Only time will tell, and I will
make choices as I go along that I deem as indispensable, relative,
and significant. The rest, I suppose, will just happen. I always
feel like I am in a fog. The minutes in discovering clarity seem
heavily sedated. I am impatient and restless.

*Journal*
September 16, 2012

I am ravenous for something that I know is no good and I'm
tired of being so tactful in my upstanding morals. I want to
be intoxicated with this insatiable desire. I want it to overtake
me. I want to be away from my mind of righteousness and let
the vortex of passion take me. I want to be carnal and preyed
upon and seized. I want a savage command. I don't want him
to let up. I want him to pursue my inner depth and blow my
mind and body like I've never felt before.

   And then there is this short and very taunt leash of rigid
reality that pulls me back into this demanding voice that
grounds me, disciplines me, and forces its lock and anchoring
upon me. It tells me that I can't go there. It tries to persuade
me that my life is okay and these feelings will pass. This actually pisses me off! Fuck, makes me so angry. The so-called
goodness almost feels like a poison that keeps me heavily tran-
quilized and I struggle to be detoxicated. This is so backward.
Detoxicated from a poisonous goodness? What is this that

teases my mind with this haunting fascination? What is this other side of me that literally screams at me, provokes me, and dares me? Although I want, I am in a looming, disorienting confusion of "What the fuck am I thinking?" What the fuck is wrong with me? I feel like part of me is a tempest. But damn, baby, oh baby, baby, *baby*. The tempest is rattling her cage fiercely, and the louder she rattles the more convinced I am that I want to be taken. I think I need a tattoo.

We do not regret the things we did ... we regret the things we did not do.

There is a charm about the forbidden that makes it unspeakably desirable.

—Mark Twain

The only way to get rid of temptation is to yield to it.

—Oscar Wilde

*Journal*
September 28, 2012

I have met some interesting people in my life, even in the past year. One, though, is a standout. This man, who believes in a deeper comprehension of existence such as old souls, as I do, thinks we have known each other before. Nobody has ever said this to me with such conviction. Most are afraid of how stupid that might sound in such a need-for-acceptance society. Not him. Complete and perfect confidence and solid demeanor. I feel this energy alluring. His energy. It is strong and compelling. Maybe this person could have some significance in my life since I have regarded him as a standout? That is rare for me to even call someone a standout. Maybe the significance is just the intellectual dialogue that I so crave? Perhaps he will leave a mark on my history or vice versa? Whatever it is or is not, I am most unexpectedly ignited. Never felt like this. This is a new experience inside, yet he seems familiar in a mysterious type of way.

Several years ago, while going through a stressful time, I had a life-altering dream. I don't remember the entire content of the dream, but when I woke up, I felt incredibly light. I had an overwhelming sense of love surging through my entire being. I lay there trying to recall who in my dream loved me that completely, that wholly, that perfectly. I demanded to know, as there was nothing remotely comparable. I racked my brain over and over again before opening my eyes and losing my dream clarity, desperately begging, *Who are you? Who are you?* I pressed and pleaded and prayed. Then my mind fell silent and still. In the most tranquil delivery, the answer came: "It is you."

The moment was so profound, I wept into a radiant awareness. I understood I needed no one to love me outside of my own being. I had enough. I felt enlightened. I felt new, yet a complete person. As if I had been reborn, intact with aged wisdom. I felt an immense amount of implicit joy and contentment that couldn't be rationalized, debated, persuaded, or broken. Nothing, and I mean *nothing*, could impair what seemed to be a revelation. An epiphany. People took notice quite quickly. All around me, I was unaffected by the day-to-day woes or worries of distraction. I experienced light and love in its most sterling presence. This high lasted that intently for a good six weeks. I will never forget it. I cannot forget it. Now, I need it. I need to utilize it.

It is written that when the Buddha went to meditate and seek enlightenment he was there, under a tree, far into his travels, for days and days. When he awakened, he was filled with laughter, realizing that the search was not somewhere but inside himself all along.

My favorite writings are from Ralph Waldo Emerson. This one in particular struck a chord after my experience:

> Our faith comes in moments. Burn the lessons of those few hours into our minds. We have to hold onto the perspective and clarity we achieve at our peaks and let them sustain us when we are less inspired. There is depth in those brief moments.

It has been said that passions are connections to your God. I don't think we need to try so hard in life to find happiness or find God or go searching for answers as much as we think, just like the story of Buddha. The more "lightened up" I get, the more things seem to flow, capitulating to a trust that links it to a peace that was there all the while. I like that.

*Journal*
Late September 2012

I am fighting, and I am losing. I want him to take me mercilessly without warning and without leniency. I want his raw and graphic intensity to shatter my innocence with unconcealed want and not stop until he has brought me to a level of satisfying exhaustion. I don't want to feel remorse. Nor do I want to feel a resolution. I just want an experience that isn't just a taunting thought. Why? How can I possibly upset this character of mine for something that I know is not from a foundation of goodness and that also could be wildly addicting? Is this a lesson of temptation that I have to learn and overcome? Will I fail? Will I be educated? Why do I now feel like this is a necessity? I can feel a reckless magnetism to something vicious in or around me, and *fuck*, man, I am on fire. I need to be restrained. Oh man, that even turns me on. My thoughts are pulling me away. Am I being disassembled, or am I allowing a new dimension of discovering untouched corners of my essence that have always existed and will not cease its timely eruption?

> To burn with desire and keep quiet about it is the greatest punishment we can bring on ourselves.
> —Federico Garcia Lorca

I don't ever want to waste this precious life. Not long ago, I was in a place that I was seeking too much, again. I don't want to be in that place. It's too confusing and deprives from the now. I like to feel life breathe through me in its most natural continuity. I don't want to try so hard to mimic perfection or allow myself to be sloppy. I just want to open up myself to the validity of all me (not be so guarded) and try it all out, tactfully and preferably honorable. If anything comes my way that feels wrong, then it is. If I am drawn to it, I most likely need it for something. I think it can be simple yet rousing with adventure if we just let it come without fighting to control it or cowardly resisting it so much.

*Journal*
October 15, 2012

My husband is increasingly suspicious of me. He is withdrawing more into this strange, dark place in life, with low self-confidence, with more destructive money choices, his job (or, more accurately, lack of a job), and us. There is a subtle guilt that lingers within me. In the past, I would be that rock of support that a loving, decent, and supportive wife would deliver during this rough patch in his life. I am guilty of self-evolutionary visions and personal fantasies of sex and wildness going on privately inside, but I have been virtuous for all our marriage as well as through our long courtship. I feel such an unfairness, almost insulted by his pervasive suspicions, which are, in reality, unwarranted. He actually is frightening me with the way he looks at me with so much misgiving. His eyes are almost wicked and vile and corrupt. I admit I am afraid of this look. I don't want this to scare or intimidate me, but who am I kidding? We are obviously in very strained marital circumstances and have been for some time, more than I care to admit. Maybe he strongly foresees me becoming completely detached (or somehow has broken into my very private daydreams, which are so secluded in my mind). I ache for solitude, and now he looks over my shoulder all the time at what I am writing, texting—who I am talking to, where I am going, who I am seeing. This is so strange. Also, every facet of his struggles come my way in a hyper-focused need to find blame and fault in anyone other than himself. There is no accountability on his part. He is always the "victim," and I am struggling to work through challenges with him and mostly with myself and how I can be better but not lose my pertinent direction. I feel the slow severing of us. I have lost my enchantment about a fairy tale marriage, retiring now to the belief that maybe the propulsion of passion is, in fact, ephemeral and everything including romantic love, has a shelf life. I have given everything of myself to this marriage and to him, and I really wanted to receive love and compassion from him and for him to pay attention to us not in quantity but in quality. I had asked for only a little of his time, just a moment of caliber benevolence here and there so we could keep our relationship growing. I was worth it. *We* were worth it. He was absent and remained absent. This neglect, his ongoing irresponsibility, his significant lies and his deepening darkness, which I know that I cannot fix, and my changing at the same fucking time are *not* resonating. I loved him deeply and always will, but we both have fallen out from each other. I know that I am responsible for my own direction, and I will choose how to respond to circumstances, both good and bad. Respond, not react to all circumstances. I am getting older every day. I want no regrets. I want to rock this decade. I want to rock my life. Am I all that I can be? For him as well as for myself?

> Whosoever is delighted in solitude is either a wild beast or a god.
> —Aristotle

> Guard your spare moments. They are like uncut diamonds. Discard them and their value will never be known. Improve them and they will become the brightest gems in a useful life.
> —Ralph Waldo Emerson

In lieu of all this disorder, I do like this personal transit with its inevitable direction of self-growth and the sense of an audacious advancement that I am drawn to. I have work to do here on this planet. It may be just for my own self-satisfaction, or maybe I have gifts to offer this world that would not only be fascinating to me but highly rewarding. I have no idea, but I do know that I can't be stopped. I am already in this. I am so very excited about the movement of life, even if I am alone.

What we do in life echoes in eternity.

—*Gladiator*

All you can do in life is be who you are. Some will love you for you. Most will love you for what you can do for them, and some won't like you at all.

—Rita Mae Brown

Am I all that I can be?

# PART 2
## *Falling In*

My heart is afraid it will have to suffer, the boy told the alchemist one night as they looked up at the moonless sky, "Tell your heart that the fear of suffering is worse than the suffering itself. And that no heart has ever suffered when it goes in search of its dreams …He also values his freedom very highly, which is why he became a Shepard and why he is reticent to get involved in things which threaten his freedom. In the end, he realizes that playing it safe is often more threatening to his freedom than taking a risk."

—Paulo Coelho, *The Alchemist*

*Journal*
October 2012

The connection with this man I spoke of earlier, in September, is very unusual. It is unusual because it is so comfortable. If there is such thing as past lives, as we discussed, then we must have had some kind of encounter between us. I know some find this corny and stupid, but I believe in this, or at least I want to for its romantic and magical appeal. I sense a unique closeness unlike anything I have experienced thus far—enigmatic, stimulating. Many people deny the deep mystical as it is run purely on a faith of heart, not on the practicality of fact, but so is anything that is beyond. This is why I love it so much. I do not particularly need fact from science to prove things. Trusting my deepest self has been the only proof I have needed or that is worth anything to me. My soul connects to this man. It is "beyond," and I am moved and lifted by him.

A soulmate is an ongoing connection with another individual that the soul picks up again in various times and places over lifetimes. We are attracted to another person at a soul level not because that person is our unique complement, but because by being with that individual, we are somehow provided with an impetus to become whole ourselves.

—Edgar Cayce

Do you think that the Universe fights for souls to be together? Some things are too strange and strong to be coincidences.

—Emery Allen

I don't have a large quantity of friendships. I do pick my friends attentively. I do not want anyone in my circle of energy that distracts me from what I deem as meaningful and purposeful. I am not trying to be pompous and arrogant, but who you hang around is extremely influential. I am sensitive to people's energy and what people carry. I have privately rejected certain types of company so I do not deter from my highest possible progression, and I am certain I have been rejected as well for those same reasons or for other reasons personal to that individual. All is fine by me. Maybe friends just find one another by means of a connection that all souls simply find inevitable. For one reason or another, all have been very significant people, even the ones I had to let go or they let go of me at some point in our timeline. The dignity and acceptance of a final farewell that does not include a physical death of the individual but the necessary death of the relationship itself have been of the utmost importance in learning lessons within the dynamics of a collective wholeness for however long or short the affinity requires. Longevity is inconsequential. Substance is everything.

This connection with him is getting more pronounced. It started when I began to notice him working out in a local gym (one of several that I attend). I don't pay too much attention to people in the gym because I am there for disciplinary demands on my body. I do not socialize there, and often, I have headphones in even with no music to deter conversation. However, on occasion, I would randomly listen to conversations around me and, on even more rare occasions, engage. He was arrogant in a mesmerizing appeal, annoying but with a charismatic draw, odd in an artistic twist. Getting into brief conversations with him was stimulating to me. He was different. He would ask some random question that would take me off guard, and I began to enjoy the play of banter and far-fetched discourse and discussion. This was not defined by me as flirting, as I found him unattractive in the physical sense. However, his odd and quirky differences were enlivening to me. It became refreshing, exciting, and somewhat intellectually provocative, but all the while, there was that familiar and comfortable awareness.

One day, he asked me if I taught my children all "this" (the discipline of working out). I told him, "I don't sit them down and talk teach anything. I hope to teach by example alone." Although this was no deep insight, he suddenly stared at me without reply with a slight and agreeable smile. The way he looked at me at that moment, I felt he looked entirely past my eyes, my words, and directly into my soul as we then communed in a lock I have never experienced. It touched me. I was almost embarrassed, thinking he must have recognized my surprise by his deep reach. As I relaxed with it, I felt an even richer affinity to this strange yet fascinating man.

The older fun group of people at the gym asked me to attend their weekly happy hour one night. I never attend these, but a girlfriend who also attended this gym didn't want to show up alone. He surprisingly showed up a little later. There, we were able to talk more, and he told me words that bewildered me: "I know you," he stated rather directly. He "knows" me? This took me aback, as I was chilled with his words identical to my unexposed thoughts. I replied confidently but secretly bemused, "Yes, you do." We were inseparable from conversation the rest of that night, completely glued as we talked and laughed with ease and grace.

One morning at the gym, the old fun guys were having a discussion about the freedom to converse with the opposite sex while having a girlfriend or wife and without the possessive lock of feeling threatened by senseless suspicions from them. He was listening in on the conversation, and he leaned over to me and asked, "Would your husband feel threatened?" A couple of days later, I responded via email (which was given out during that happy hour for a "next happy hour" group interest), apologizing for my abrupt exit as I was left without comment to his question. His response after my quick email apology mesmerized me with its use of the "dropped back in" remark.

> For whatever reason you "dropped back in," since there are no coincidences, it can only be for the very best of reasons. I do not understand certain things, probably most things, and don't apologize, at least not to me. It is not necessary. Things get complicated all on their own, I will never add to that. So at least when you are around me, CHILL.

> Dax

> I finally answered the question I walked away from:

> Should he feel threatened?

> Because I have a sincere loyalty to those I love and I have a more sincere loyalty to my character and he (my husband) knows this, things are deemed safe. However, I have come to change my mind about certain issues, and I am intensely crazy and wild about my life and the experiences that my soul shouts at me to pay attention to. Husbands like wives to be home to take care of them and the family and their house. I have a hunger to travel and talk deeply to other people, to discover more about other souls I connect with, not because I am

missing something from him but because I have a fascination with uniqueness of individual expression, which intrigues me to go deeper. I have been domesticated, and during the time my children were little, it was fine. Now, it is unsustainable. Domesticated—how utterly poisonous to the wild. My children are still in need of me, and I have a job to willingly complete, but I am on *fire* with adventure and self-discovery. The thing that matters most to me are making sure that my kids are on track for a happy life and that I have given them enough foundation to carry on independently. Simultaneously, I want to feed my soul with what it is I am supposed to do with my own personal growth and happiness. I thrive on this potential adventure and happiness. I am genuinely spiritual and think all sorts of crazy shit most of my days, but it's this crazy shit that excites me and drives me forward. No complacency can reside in my being for long. Some are threatened by that because I can't be controlled or subdued. I'm not sure I do believe in an entire predetermined *life* or not. I think I am more of a believer that we create our days or moments around given (predetermined) *lessons* we need for the thrust to move forward. I won't deny myself a possible lesson from any experience if its intensity keeps coming at me time and time again. I think it's the universe's way of saying do not fear me; experience me. It's going to keep coming until it's learned anyway. I like that. Hey, you asked. Don't you know this already since you know me?

Jade

His reply:

I *completely* understand. *Completely.* You described me, and none of it scares me. Not following through does, and I do not want to waste time. I am surprised by this response; I won't be ever again.

Since I been focusing on my spiritual life. Answers and people have been funneled into my life almost as needed. When faced with difficult problems, the answers were given to me during meditation. When I presented the solutions, people were left speechless. I was given credit for things that were from "divine sources," not my imagination. So, I have come to trust what is "sent" to me. In twenty-two plus years of marriage, I have never had a comparable "pull," so when one came it was interesting, uncomfortable, and confusing. Attraction is common. I have had numerous opportunities to meet attractive women. I get teased about it, but I never came close to straying. But this time, the shit did not go away, and I did not understand it. You are attractive but do not appear spiritual. Therefore, I was saying, what is going on? I tried to dismiss it, couldn't, and then tried again. It kept pulling me toward you. Attractive but not spiritual, so blow this off. No such luck. The pull got stronger. Then, I said something the other day to you, and your answer moved me. Then I got to talk to you, and I realized there was way more to you than good "abs." If this is freaking you out, I understand. But I am cool with it as it is happening for a reason. It is beyond me. I am surprised at your answer because you hide that part of your life. People know that I think as I do. Those that don't, don't matter. Serving is the only thing that gives me moments of pleasure. The more I can do for others, the more I want to do. I do not live vicariously through my children. I do not want my wife to be a housewife, do chores, take care of me. God forbid. I could never allow that, could not live with it. She deserves better than that, is better than that. I want all those around me to excel but to do so with compassion for others. Like you, my legacy to my family is by example, not lecture. I am nowhere near done; I am more motivated than ever. I am a seeker.

I have been given experience and gifts. I did not earn them or deserve them. I want to make sure that I use them appropriately. "They" say that *God* created death so life would have more meaning. Life is a gift. I attack it. I always have tried to dream big and achieve. *God* is never glorified when we think small. Why you have "dropped back in" has to be for a reason. I accept that but will *never* compromise you or me or make you uncomfortable with my "stuff." To me, this is cool, but if you are uncomfortable with this or me, just say it.

Why am I surprised? "The pull" was so strong, it threw me. Now I get it. I decided to send you this in advance so you had time to decide to blow me off or not or see where this goes. Curiously, who do you share your inside "stuff" with? How many people on this planet know what you shared with me? How many people know what you think about?

Dax

My reply:

Most people are afraid. I am not (or at least trying not to be). Sometimes, I share with a select few that I am close to, but I am tactful in my delivery. Some of these individuals are very old, wise souls that made the sharing easy. New souls (if you believe in that sort of thing) seem fragile, and I want to get into their depth by sharing, but often, there is a wall of human protection likely called the "ego" encased in the illusion of fear. So, lately, sharing is limited. You asked me how many people know what I think about? Currently, no one but you. I felt a kinship inclusive of depth and understanding almost immediately with you that feels uncommonly safe. You fascinate me. I am moved by your direct response in email and impressed by your measure of character and more impressed by your inner wisdom. As previously mentioned, we surely must know each other from "before," *if* there really is such a thing, or if it just something I choose to believe in because I like it and its cool because it's deep. Thus, connection is backed by something more enchanting. Who knows? Don't really care, but since we both understand and resonate with the "dropped back in," I also feel there is reason for our connection that likely should not be ignored. I know that we are not supposed to know everything until time is weaved into matter. It is frustrating to most humans, as we want it all now, but patience is imperative. I try not to figure things out so I can let life nudge me along with hints as I create steps forward that are necessary for me. We have a mind, a body, and a soul. Most let their minds control most of their lives (i.e., falling into lusting sexual affairs out of mere temptation), some let their bodies decide (many won't leave the house if there is an impending physical ailment). For others and definitely myself, the soul is the master of thy being. It drives me to discipline both mind and body. It is the ultimate commander of my center. I trust it with all that I am. That is why, if there is an experience that beckons my attention again and again and again, I better start listening. I don't know why we connected, but I suppose it is not time to understand it quite yet. You must know, though, that I have no intention of hurting anyone, complicating anyone's life, or causing someone distress. I am here to lift people up. I am certain of that. If I hurt anyone, it would slowly chip away at the very character I am proud of. When I am alone with my thoughts, I better not have the need to escape myself. Although lately, my mind is rustling up a boatload of issues, I am trying to make sense of and calm it the fuck down. That is another topic altogether. As far as "this," I know that you and I are already close. Maybe it is a small thing like me teaching you to listen since you do tend to talk way too much (ha ha), or maybe you are supposed to teach me to *chill* (since I am restless). Regardless, we are already in each other's lives, like it or not. I suppose, we will eventually figure it out.

By the way, I never have hidden the spiritual part of myself. I don't hide at all. We are at the gym, and it's hard to talk there when my focus is trying to keep my body from its ageing declination.

Jade

Our writing continues on a daily basis, as if it is imperative. I look so forward to seeing his name pop up in my inbox like a little girl all giddy with her first crush. I pause briefly to think about how silly this is. I like the silliness. I like the playfulness. It feels harmless. I feel no wrong. I feel light. I feel ... something.

October 2012

Dear Dax,

I know that I am part of something bigger. Whether you call it God, spirit, or universe, it makes no difference. I'm not a

regular at any church or organization, as I am a nonconform-
ist. I know that in order to obtain the magic of it all, you need
simply to be open. I know that there is a power greater than
all of us, and it is available to use and accept it as we choose.
There is no actual judgement but what we allow ourselves
to judge and our story around it. I live an ordinary life, yet
with complex depth, which, in turn, gives me exceptional
moments, which are keys to my happiness. I know that the
people you meet are important and all part of one's "personal
legend" (from one of my favorite books, *The Alchemist*). Some
for a minute and others for a lifetime. I know we have more
than one soulmate. Never close a door to those who are your
soulmates, because without their insight and love and acceptance and trust, there will be a missing link or void in your
life. I know that I may get uncomfortable in situations, but I
want to embrace the discomfort, get my head away from the
situation, so I can hear my soul speak for ultimate clarity. I
can't say I am here to provide a service to the world, like you,
but I know I am here, as we all are, for the discovery of depth
and magnitude and beauty of the divine intensity that resides
in each and every one of us. I want life to pour into me. I
want to experience me. I want to experience you. I want to
experience everything that calls to me without regret, without
hesitation, without fear. I know that I can feel right and I can
feel wrong. I sense things before they happen, not always, but
often. I know that I need to open that up more. I know that
each and every day is a glorious opportunity to just play in it.
I know I do not want to take things too seriously because the
lighter I am, the clearer things seem to become. I know that
today, in all its beauty that I am really tired, as I don't do well
without sleep, but I will force myself out of this box and let
the sun speak to me about living and carry me through and
onward. Then, when the awesomeness of night falls, I will
go out and look at the vast sky, raise my glass, and thank the

universe for all it has given to me and hope that tonight, I will have a peaceful sleep. I am drawn to circumstances that I do not yet understand, but sometimes that's okay because there is a time for everything, and letting go for me is difficult, but trusting (so far in this life) is not. I know I need to get a handle on my fantasy shit before I completely go mad. It's crazy what I imagine. There is so much more to know about me, about life, about the totality of it all. It is never-ending fascination.

Jade

He responded,

Those things that you are now experiencing, wild and free, should never have been contained. As soon as you recognized their presence, you should have let them fly. How can that be wrong?

Dax

I respond,

I like to write in my journal to release a part of me that I keep private from everyone else. Why? Because often if I attempt to share, no one is really interested in listening. Also, some of it would hurt people and I know it, but it is still part of me that I want and need to express. I don't believe in shutting off part of yourself because someone else has a problem with it, but I don't want to throw it in their face because I have deep respect and empathy for their feelings beyond a normal compassion. It sounds like a contradiction, but I know the truth of myself. I want to be genuine with all aspects of myself, and sometimes, that remains in my private realm. The more open the person is on the receiving end (should I share) without trying to fix or mold me into their design, the more open I am. I am protective of my intentions. There is a portal to the soul in every individual. It's that openness of trust and acceptance and love that allows a free ride into mine. The moment is all we have, but everything in your life matters. It is all encompassing.

Jade

He responds,

Some time, when we *can*, we will sit and talk. That will help. You do not have a problem. Neither do I. I trust you and that is very hard for me. I trust you without good reason, that is impossible for me, but I do. I am not confused by that.

Dax

How can we interpret one another with so much precision and at such ease like this? It seems completely natural in the most unnatural of circumstance. I was in church the other day and a line in the minister's message was so spiritually astute.

> Sometimes if we don't pay attention to things in our life that are necessary for our own personal evolvement, the universe has no other resources than to push us in. Life wants us to flow.

I am not by any means advocating people going out and attempt to fill emptiness by searching for new love or companionship somewhere else because their home life is unsatisfying or for whatever reason. That is not who I am. However, I am convinced, or want to be convinced, that the relevance of this "relationship" is pertinent to both of us. I feel encouraged within to let this ride.

> A soul connection is a resonance between two people who respond to the essential beauty of each other's individual natures, behind their facades, and who connect on this deeper level. This kind of mutual recognition provides the catalyst for a potent alchemy. It is a sacred alliance whose purpose is to help both partners discover and realize their deepest potentials. While a heart connection lets us appreciate those we love just as they are, a soul connection opens up a further dimension--seeing them for who they could be, and for who we could become under their influence. This means recognizing that we both have an important part to play in helping each other become more fully who we are. ... A soul connection not only inspires us to expand, but also forces us to confront whatever stands in the way of that expansion.
> —John Welwood

> Avoid the company of persons with whom you cannot be totally forthright. Be sincere or be silent. Speak the whole truth, as you see it, or do not speak at all.
> –Ralph Waldo Emerson

I am refreshed in spirit conversing with this man of great sagacity and intuition. No doubt, we are akin both in measures of seeking the soul and mere common interests in mind. I can't help but wonder if our bodies would connect in the deepest of intimacy? I think of this, of course, with my on-going and outlandish foolish brain, that is full of insatiable and immature daydreams with a nameless/faceless person. I know that I shouldn't be writing back and forth like this. I am drawn to the magnetism but torn, allowing guilt to ride my wing at the herald of compromise. This is something so unusual for me and so unexpected. Or have I created this, and I am rationalizing it all out of irrational and ignorant surface infatuation or pathetic loneliness I have slightly hidden within the word boredom? I ask for clarity and guidance. I ask for truth. I pray more than I ever have. I resent logic and invite my heart to lead this. Was I this hollow in my life? Was I? Have I deeply hidden my hurt in life?

> Three things are not long hidden ... the sun, the moon, and the Truth.
>                                   —Buddha

I am of strong opinion that universal truth is woven into our souls before we are born, which is why we sense the differences between goodness and not so good (which some call evil or sin), and why we are motivated at points in our lives (especially midlife) to master current talents and give birth to new creativity that we likely long suppressed, even if it seems obscure. It must be innate. The divinity within each person knows this at a core level, yet different upbringings, experiences, and cultural influences often cause people to be dazed or sidetracked—but seemingly it still dwells. I want to listen to the knowing within; stillness speaks and wisdom resides. I am certain this must be true.

I was reading a book on the law of attraction, and it had this statement in it:

Many believe that the meaning they give to their experiences are real. Your interpretation of life events is based on your past experiences, beliefs, and upbringing. Realize that your interpretation of the situation is something you have made up. It is all a creation of your mind. You actually have the power to choose what feelings you attach to each situation, event and experience.
—Sonia Ricotti, *The Law of Attraction, Plain and Simple*

Oh, man, this is both mind fucking and fucking exciting. I am not sure about all this. What exactly is real within the realm of your perception? What is real at all?

Lately, people have shared stories about infidelity, darkness, depression, divorce, and lack of integrity. It is disturbing. Got a call from my best friend from seventh grade today, as she was going through some serious life-altering shit with her husband, and listening to her made me cringe. She spoke of her desire to have a sexual affair with a friend we went to high school with out of a desperate lack of attention as well as a lack of intimacy. So many people seem aimlessly lost. I am not lost, or at least do not feel lost. So many people are sad and depressed, with so many problems. I am not depressed, although I can definitely feel sad, and maybe I am, in fact, unfulfilled. I am thinking, thinking of my own life and how I will compose it. We are so powerful and can be absolute fools with that power. I want to rise against the outside bullshit and trust my inside movement. I don't want to be mediocre. I want to have noteworthy moments every day, without compromise, without penitence, without hurting others, and without any fucking chance that I deter myself and chance the admission of darkness because I didn't have the courage to try. I need the light to thrive within.

As I think of these ideas, I want to share it with only one person. I think of him here and there, and I look forward to talking with him when he gets back from a distant trip and being around his tremendous light.

He writes,

We are not fools. We are often deceived. I do not believe in predestiny. I believe in karma. You create both positive light and darkness. Is it a good thing or a bad thing? What is good and what is bad. By definition, I have been both. Really, I am neither. I am me. It is a constant struggle to stay *me*. You said earlier, "Are you playing a game with yourself?" No, this is complicated. Opinions fly. *People become estranged. Victims are created.* Why, to justify the logic other people apply to the situation? "We do *not* see things the way they are, we see them the way *we* are," says Anais Nin. Consequently, every opinion we have is based on what, our life experiences? So, what type of experience do most people have? Those that are traditionally safe? Let me hear from an experienced person that knows victory and defeat, has laughed hard and cried hard, stood tall and crawled. A person that has lived as both a lion and a lamb. Now there is someone worth getting some *advice* from. Safe? What is that, a toothless tiger? We are better than that. If I fail, let me fail on the biggest stage, where everyone knows of my failure. But this is *not* about public opinion. This is about the importance of our lives and what we do with them. We are godlike. Let's act like it.

Stop listening to everybody else. Let your soul speak to you, but you have to be still. I know that is not your thing. Got to keep moving. Ski fast, run fast, move your body. I got that and admire it. On occasion, slow down and listen to your soul.

Let it tell you who you are and why you are here. Your inner voice is all you need to listen to, not your desires, needs, goals, whatever. Your inner voice. Get counseling from the *universe*. It speaks. Are you listening?

Dax

I respond,

I try to be still when I am in bed right before I have to get out in the morning. It's that moment where I am coming off the subconscious tunnel into the conscious. Amazing things happen there. I can get to ten minutes, and then my brain turns on and my body gets excited about the wake of the morning. I am trying to be still and learn from the silence while sitting still, but as you noticed, it's hard. I do like the effect after I run. It takes about thirty minutes post-run for my high to kick in, but right when I am done, I am weary and peaceful, and it's a good gateway to that serene place of undisturbed silence, where messages seem to be sent and dreams seem to be heard. I know, I know. It's not the same, but it's a start. You can help me with that.

Jade

*Journal*
Late October 2012

The sexual potency that charges through me often is more powerful than I know what to do with. It scares me more because it has become more, and I'm not sure if I can tame the pull of its ferocity. Why do I dare continue to tempt the raw and impatient desires that are flooding my mind? I am now insatiable. The thoughts are haunting me, yet I want them to torment. They cause distraction, yet I want the disturbance. They could cause harm, yet I want the danger. This is dark, and I am being allured. I have impeccable character, but I cannot stop.

As mentioned, I have always had phenomenal sex with my husband, but now I have completely removed myself from it while I am still carrying on within it. I do not feel secure with him to let myself go at all, as I did in the past. I feel a need to heavily insulate my feelings and tuck away from this marriage so that I can prepare. What? Did I just write this? Prepare? Prepare for what? What the fuck? I try to come back to him, but I feel self-vacated. I feel desolate. I feel abandoned, but am I *not* the one doing the abandoning? My trust is bereft, and I feel the dichotomy of being orphaned by a relationship I thought was solid in longevity and the illumination of a spark of newness in the mysticism within my very essence that is *more* than captivating. And in the very near thought ... is him.

I don't want to stop this writing and talking. I am drawn to it as if it is too paramount in significance to deny or delay its continuance. I try to insist that I am doing nothing wrong. It's just writing and connecting. I rationalize my repugnant behavior but allow a flawed reprieve. I feel alive, though. I feel again, and there can't be anything bad about that. Look at me, trying to justify myself. This embarrasses my own self. In reality (logical, practical, reasonable), we are being disloyal to the commitment of marriage, with our families, with our character. This tugs gravely on my integrity and on my morale, yet I persist. I persist voraciously. I can't tear myself away. It's too strong, and passion for life and perhaps passionate love resonates from my soul. I am inundated with stamina and bold tenacity.

Delay is the deadliest form of denial.
                    —C. Northcote Parkinson

"But how will I know who my soul mate is?"
"By taking risks," Wicca said to Brida. "By
risking failure, disappointment, disillusion,
but never ceasing in your search for love. As
long as you keep looking, you will triumph in
the end."
                    —Paulo Coelho, Brida

I have studied spiritualism, and throughout the years, I
have come to adopt the belief that we have spiritual guides
as well as spiritual soulmates in our lives. Soul guides could
be many people/acquaintances throughout your life, but for
short periods of time. We have strong connections with our
soul guides but an incontestable prophecy of perfected unity
with our soulmates. There is no denying your intense pull toward these deep individuals. You know them. You feel them.
You want to immerse yourself in one another, not out of attachment but out of elevation. Soulmates come into your life
and remain for the duration of your life's journey. There is
a profound love, unmatched yet ever growing. Familiar yet
fresh with the excitement of new discovery and evolvement.
A soulmate may need you, or you will need something from
them, but the togetherness is an unbeatable empowerment.

Love is composed of a single soul inhabiting
two bodies.
                    —Aristotle

My husband told me how much he loved me last night.
I listened to his words, but they do not reach me. It is
heart-wrenching to feel him ache, though. My God, how

could I ever let that happen? How could I ever cause another that I love and care enormously for to ever suffer at all? How can I protect his heart? I feel detached, and I am desperate for time alone to consider how to even breathe let alone how to help others. Most often, I am anesthetized by prohibiting myself to love him uncompromised. I feel the amount of love I can give is blocked, maybe intentionally, maybe unintentionally. I want to give freely, but I am compelled to resistance, so I retract even farther out. This blocking makes me very sad because I know this is harmful to him, and it makes me feel sickened for not working harder at putting everything aside for this all to work out for him. But this resistance holds me back with a vengeance. What is this that is going on with me? I do not understand, and I do not know what to do. I am so sick of myself for this repetitive confusion. When I told my husband I could not live a complacent life, he told me that in a relationship, I need to be less selfish. He could be right, but I feel so taken all the time that I want to take this time, for the first time ever, for just me. Can I not have some space? Can I have a short sabbatical from everyone else? Is that selfish? Is it pertinent? Sometimes, I think of a different life. My husband and I had seemed to fit together in many ways, but the thought of my marriage (staying with him) is sometimes overbearing and elusive, and I crave to escape it for a while and be something/somewhere different. Perhaps this is just a stage of ebb and flow in its innocent yet typical stage of the twenty-plus years of marriage. Perhaps, I have made this all too complex by my intrigue of spirit overcharging and overriding other important yet challenging life events. To make my marriage viable, I will need to dedicate practice to make my ambitions for self-curiosity dissipate or at least grab a life vest with the intent of keeping my head above water. I do love my husband, and I deeply love my family. How can I make this all right for them without allowing myself to disappear? Expectations of my goodness and expectations of my integrity are on constant observation. In a weird, warped way, I admire people with fewer principles, fewer rules. I envy their carefree liberation. I need to resurface my intention for the sanctuary of autonomy. Who am I? Be fucking bold in it!

What is loyalty anyway? If I am loyal to my husband and resist the zealous persistence toward the "pull" in order to keep marriage/family intact then that is disloyal to my soul, and I become fraudulent because I am dishonorable to self-truth. If I am loyal to myself by honoring this pull toward change, which could lead me away, far away, then I am disloyal to my husband. Instead of seeing loyalty and honor entwined in harmonic momentum, I see loyalty and honor in the fighting ring to battle out, which should actually take the trophy of truth. If loyalty to him wins out, would he accept me if he knew I was imperfect? I can't let that happen. He deserves better. I deserve better. Deceiving my soul is the thief of honor and ultimately an inferior truth.

> If we cannot live with our need to renew agreements we have made, we break the only promise we really owe each other ... to be truthful. This means finding the courage to be truthful with ourselves and a way to live with how our actions affect others even when there is no ill intent and no one to blame.
> —Oriah, *The Invitation*

> I don't know that love changes. People change. Circumstances change.
> —Nicholas Sparks

I like the safeness and freedom that Dax has allowed me to encounter. It has become my sacred refuge. I am grateful for him coming into my life at this very moment. He allows me to be me without any attachment or expectation. I can breathe.

Whatever relationships you have attracted in your life at this moment, are precisely the ones you need in your life at this moment. There is a hidden meaning behind all events, and this hidden meaning is serving your own evolution.

—Deepak Chopra

*Journal*
November 2012

I am compelled to reach farther into his energy to recognize or discover more of him. This is not a superficial coincidence. I must vindicate my own head in this so I can explore this unity through the wisdom of my heart. Trust my heart. It has never let me down.

While attempting to let go with ease, I am becoming more rebellious and more aggressive in pulling away from anyone that takes from me, robs from me, of me. I feel the inside of me becoming relentless in the quest to be saturated and empowered with inner strength and purpose. I will no longer be controlled or owned or possessed. I will not be submissive and quell my aspirations. I am more than what they think. I am much more than what I thought.

Sometimes we fall down because there is something down there we need to find.

—Unknown

It isn't by getting out of the world that we become enlightened, but by getting into the world ... by getting so tuned in that we can ride the waves of our existence and never get tossed because we become the waves.

—Ken Kesey, *Kesey's Garage Sale*

Dear Dax,

My marriage may or may not be salvageable. However, when I think of a salvageable marriage, it feels right for him but an injustice for me and feels dishonorable to all. I want to be a good person and feel good about myself and the decisions that I make. I want the people that look up to me to see me as an example of merit and to know that those qualities are rooted for the foundation of morality to serve you in your life when other things crumble. Inside and privately, I rebel at this. I rebel because I want an untethered life and that what others might deem as good and wholesome may not be so good and wholesome for me in pursuit of the lessons I know I need in life for fulfillment and ultimate spiritual evolution, even if there is suffering involved and obstacles to overcome. I just want to have my hand on the throttle. Life is so short. It's running out. I don't want to waste time. If that means redefining my values and stepping over the no-crossing line to help me reveal direction and truth, then I may have to pursue. I am high in rebellion today. I think it is time you kiss me slowly. Let's go for a ride.

Jade

Did I just write that to him? What the *fuck?* I pressed send so quickly and so matter-of-factly. Fuck, man. Here I go. Am I going to fall in moral descent, or will I permit the rise of an admissible heart for something now deemed as unstoppable?

He responds to me,

> In a strange way, I like this complexity. It makes me feel again. I can shut down and focus on being productive. That is not working for me anymore. I can't hide behind that. One of my neighborhood boys called me yesterday and told me he was driving around because he did not want to go home. The idea of "till death do us part" made him want to throw up. My phone was ringing like crazy last night—family, business, people expecting me to jump. People want to meet with me today, an hour here, an hour there. My phone rings, and now, when it does, I cringe. *My family and my wife are not problems.* Neither am I. *Your family, your husband are not problems.* Neither are you. Stuff comes to us. Why? For a reason. Is it to test our resolve, see how long we can hold our breath? Can we stand firm? I do not think so. Fuck this.

> Dax

This takes my breath away. I examine myself closely. I question my vulnerability, and I am careful to not get infatuated and consumed with good words or clever catch lines. After bypassing this thought of paranoia or fear, I do feel that I can trust him unequivocally and my perceived authenticity of him. Fuck, I am moved.

> Life is not measured by the number of breaths we take, but by the moments that take our breath away.
>
> —Unknown

> Everything happens for a reason. Sometimes good things fall apart so better things can come together.
>
> —Marilyn Monroe

When I saw that psychic back in August, my sister was with me and wrote down everything she said. I came across it a few days ago and reread it. I am awed by the words on the paper. Did I end up creating a story through manifesting the possibility, with focused intention, to probable outcome? Could he be the one she was referring to? Is this the magical love affair? I thought an affair was all about sex. Is this labeled as an affair because of our deep talking or our interest? Our emailing? Our connection?

I did not share with him what this psychic focused on with the intensity of a card pulled that was of intertwined souls in immense love. "You will be passionately involved with this person, but he has someone else, but you will come together anyway. You will end up together." This is so bizarre and absurd. I am married. He is married. That is that. Seems inconceivable, yet it is ever so phenomenal.

> The heart has its reason for which reason knows not.
>
> —Blaise Pascal

Love makes your soul crawl out from its
hiding place.

—Z. N. Hurston

He writes,

> I have confidence in you, in your dreams.
> You are gifted. What else could you ask for
> or want? We are *not* limited by our circum-
> stances; we are challenged by them.
>
> We are changing, so as we change, so
> do the circumstances we must overcome.
> Enlightenment is a personal direction but
> should be our only goal.
>
> One ship sails east, the other west, by the
> SELF-SAME winds that blow. Tis the seat
> of the soul that determines the goal, and not
> the calm or strife.
>
> —Ella Wheeler Wilcox
>
> In essence, not circumstances, not pre-
> destiny. I love the fact I was blessed to get to
> know you ... again.
>
> Dax

I respond,

> Your words touch me. They resonate in me.
> You are close within my spirit, and I am com-
> pletely drawn to that. To you.
>
> Jade

I look at these writings. I am inclined to save them all, something I have never done with anyone except the one who captured my young heart thirty years ago. I knew then. I know now. I am frightened, and I am most inspired. Sometimes, I beg my God to make this go away. Sometimes, I pray to let it be. I want so much to be good, and I want so much to discover goodness.

> I was falling. Falling through time and space and stars and sky and everything in between. I fell for days and weeks and what felt like lifetime across lifetimes. I fell until I forgot I was falling.
>
> —Jess Rothenberg

> What you seek is seeking you.
>
> —Rumi

*Journal*
November 2012

I want to find the unspoken in him intimately, far beyond anything physical. This is crazy in all the great ways in a world that belongs only to us but such a disappointment in a real-life scenario. I had time tonight to be with him, and he couldn't. Tomorrow, I cannot. This will happen so often and will cause so much tension and longing. Ultimately, I wonder if we will be able to sustain the ongoing strain and stress while eventually facing the rational fact that we can't exist under all the demands. There is too much "real life" happening to us just to be the "us" we are now so enamored with. If I continue with him, it would be painful because we can never be in a place to love completely, wholly, vehemently. Our souls would connect even more in such rapture that there would not be a word to describe the magnitude of it. I can't let myself go there. I feel the despair pairing with painful rejection if I open that door. Could I withstand that? Tonight showed me that perhaps I need to stop this from going deeper before I allow myself to go to that place that imitates heaven, but then it could all be ripped away, and I could be left with a shattered heart and a very lonely, lost, and complicated soul in a world that impersonates hell. And yes, I will have learned, and I will grow, but I can learn and grow with practical adaptation of common fucking sense instead of letting myself go into him. This is the side of me that is the thinker/overthinking and perhaps only the egotistical, fearful human side, which has nothing to do with my inner realm. It is the logical side that barely exists in me but is still annoyingly loud. The soul side of me says something completely different. It says, "Fuck you, you shallow shell of a human." Feel deeply anyway. Love deeply and fiercely with all that you are. Take the chance. Take the risk. Fail. Get rejected. Feel loss. Grieve. Then rise up. Find your resilience. Love again and again and again and again. I do not care because I want to have experiences that move me that cause me to become awake even if for a brief moment once again. I want to lie in the sun with my soul instead of paddling in the swamp with my ego.

Don't fall in love, *rise* in *it*.

—Amit Abraham

I was not intentionally looking for this, was I? Was he? But what do we do with this? How can we do anything with it? Why did this come? Have I allowed this, generated this, dreamed this? Is this the universal law corresponding to my desire? His desire? Is this the ebb and flow of reality? Is this the hollow and barren heart that is ignited and captivated by passion? Why did love come again? Why now? Why this kind of love? Why, when my soul wants to personally expand and be free? Is love the answer to freedom? Does truth bask in the eminence of love?

In chaos there is fertility.

—Anais Nin

Love is the only freedom in the world because it so elevates the spirit that the laws of humanity and the phenomena of nature do not alter the course.

—Kahlil Gibran

Whatever happens, I promise to myself to live a life of personal euphoria. I will do whatever it takes to put this intention foremost, as well as my intention to create a foundation of happiness and safety for my children's lives, which must continue to cultivate and thrive with my outward attempt at strength and stability. I believe in taking risks, with backbone and gut. Everything has its moment. I can't be behind myself or forward. I could miss something too relevant. It has been written that "thoughts become things." I think I am becoming more of a believer in this than any other theory out there. Once mastered, this, I believe, is the key to a very successful and intensely wealthy life of refined contentment (not complacency but contentment). I want to acquire these skills and become them, so I am working in this field of disciplined direction. Faith in these thoughts become a supremacy. This is why prayer works. "The answer to prayer is within the prayer." If people pray as if it is already done, then they are manifesting their destiny. I believe it all works the same. However, repeated practice is the only way that this can come to any realization. There can be no doubt, no ambiguity—none. The laws of the universe are indisputable. Its fucking intriguing.

> The mind is everything. What you think you become.
>
> —Buddha

> Thoughts become things. If you see it in your mind, you will hold it in your hand.
>
> —Bob Proctor

The Pull

I speak of this pull a lot. I simply don't know what else to call it. Before the connection with Dax, I felt such charge for more than what I was admitting or allowing. I was so restless and impatient with this disturbance, I was constantly in discomfort by the day. Fuck, I tried reading more, writing more, running more, biking more, skiing more. I prayed in large churches, small churches, weird churches, talking to different friends, new friends, street acquaintances. I tried getting closer in my already close relationships. There was no reprieve from the push outward, and with this insatiability, my soul was persuaded with even more force, so, I stopped my attempts at searching for an outlet. Instead of being a conceited egocentric commander of my soul, I stepped way back and breathed life into myself. I slowed down, way down. In fact, much of my life became slow motion, as I became the watcher/the observer of my life. I fought with all my might within to love everything with an ardent heart. This calmed me enough to feel, what, perhaps, I was too afraid to let surface—my truth, which was heavy discontent. When I said it out loud, the gravity of this malaise came pouring out. Then, to my surprise, my essence from within this entrapment sparked dazzling light. My soul was radiant as it stepped back into place as my master, for it knew the only way for me to understand was to let me experience the lesson of the emptiness of my foolish grip and the wholeness revealed when I fell away from the arrogance of ego. It has to remind me many times, as I am dazed by the heaviness of circumstance. I am not the circumstances in my life; I am life within the circumstances, which simply come and go.

Everything around me started to become exciting, as if the world was mine to do whatever I wanted. I continued to retract my human self/ego and let my soul overtly rule. The amount of self-confidence was unlike anything I have ever experienced. I felt invincible. I felt love from the inside out. I felt I could do no wrong, even if it appeared that I was wrong on the outside. My mother was worried about this "change," my husband was still trying to rein me in, my friends were perplexed and some uneasy—some even walked away—and *everyone* had an opinion, but nothing was going to deter me from the way. My soul breathed immortality. I was "becoming," and this was the most rewarding thing I had felt personally in a long time. Then, he came—with the enthralling writings and limited yet precious time together to talk. My soul, on an impetus to push outward and up, had company with my blazing heart. The pull, with all its extraordinary, awe-inspiring facets driving me forward, roused me from a very dark sleep.

> I have immortal longings in me.
>                                         —Shakespeare

He has given me a bracelet blessed by his cherished guru, which he has worn for years. He puts them on my wrist, and he says, "They are for you. They are meant for you. I am certain of this." I know how important they are to him, as I have never seen him without them on his wrist. I am in the highest of gratitude and honor, and they will remind me of him and his heart. Wearing them, I feel him close to me in the night, and I wonder if he can feel me. The proximity seems inseparable.

Oh, brother, I wonder if I am just engulfed in a sick quintessential crush that it swallowed up my head. I mean, look at the shit I write. What the *fuck*? I want to bang my head against a steel door until I am more prudent. I wonder if he is like this. I embarrass my own self at the level of this infusion that has seemingly made me a possible nutcase, or maybe I am engulfed in the extraordinary, which has made me realize the rooted and real meaning of awareness and its translucent knowing of accepting love at its optimal delivery. Nutcase or awareness? Whatever this is, I admit that I like what it is bringing out in other relevant areas of myself, which are growing because of our encounter. Is this relationship a stepping-stone? A catalyst to uncover truth? A bridge to simply gain momentum? Is my heart the gateway for expansion?

> It is the soul's duty to be loyal to its own desires. It must abandon itself to its master passion.
>
> —Rebecca West

I once heard a bold statement that intrigued me with wonder. "What are relationships for? Relationships are meant to enhance the human experience." *Enhance the human experience.* I contemplate my marriage. How incredible it was to have had such a dramatic romantic experience with someone at such a young age and to have the opportunity later to have a family together. I marvel at it all. Some only dream of this and go to their grave never having had the opportunity to experience young, innocent love, or perhaps having the opportunity but not allowing the receptivity of love to come within. I have changed. All things that once experienced a rush of vitality have a mortal limit, and there is an urgency to grieve at its now steady but inevitable fatality. My heart struggles. My mind tries to persuade and then stops. Its asks, *Are you sure? Perhaps you will reconnect? Perhaps you should try even harder, with more deliberate focus.* Yet, the deep inside of me says, *No. It is done. It's time to move on.* This relationship no longer enhances. It lingers. It tethers and anchors me to something I can no longer be or perhaps never was. It was exhaustible. I never in a million years would have thought that was remotely possible.

I deem passion essential. Passion. I love the way it rolls off my tongue. I love the way it makes me ignite by mere vocalization. I love the way it looks when I write it. That one word that you invite but have no control over its launch of momentum or its inevitable fading. Love has its way of aligning itself on your journey. Passion is the pinnacle of ultimate love. Being in love—that crazy, romantic, blazing kind of love—transforms a grounded life into a capstone life. Passion in my marriage has expired. I desperately want to move on, alone. I do. I want to climb above the hilltop to the mountaintop. I want to soar from the highest peak, unattached and unescorted.

You have no obligation in relationship. You only have opportunity. Opportunity, not obligation, is the cornerstone of religion, the basis of all spirituality. So long as you see it the other way around, you will have missed the point. Relationship-your relationship-to all things was created as your perfect tool in the work of the soul. That is why all human relationships are sacred ground. It is why every personal relationship is holy. In this, many churches have it right. Marriage is a sacrament. But not because of its sacred obligations. Rather, because of its unequalled opportunity. Never do anything in a relationship out of a sense of obligation. Do whatever you do out of a sense of the glorious opportunity your relationship affords you to decide, and to be, WHO YOU REALLY ARE.

—Neale Donald Walsch, *Conversations with God*

I glanced back at the emails Dax, and I had written and things I wrote in my journal even prior to our connection. Astonishing parallels in my wants and desires, watching and acknowledging things come into actualization. It burns in my conscience to try to understand myself and my crafted life and how to make sense of a master synergy and how it all threads into a grand design. I can't make sense. I can only act from the deepest self. I refuse to act on a surface, negligent, or impatient level. I'm too much of a conscientious thinker/self-creator and have such a focus on being the very best example I can be. But now look at me. How appalling and despicable. I am not much of an example, with my collapsed integrity. For some odd and perhaps esoteric reason, I do not feel a conventional guilt or rue. I am so motivated with exploring, not only with this apparent soulmate but mostly with my endeavors toward personal discovery, with such commitment that old parts of myself are now becoming a near blur. I feel as if I am shedding layers of the decayed and burning them to ash and allowing the emergence of new self-birth and resurrected purpose, like the phoenix. I want to reach out and grasp purpose and de-mand its secrets, but it is still not close enough for the clutch.

The wild woman rises like a phoenix from the ashes of her life, to become the heroine of her own LEGEND.

—Shikoba

In order to rise from its own ashes, a phoenix must first burn.

—Octavia E. Butler

I wake in a nightmare with disillusioned thoughts. I get out of bed and have to walk around, trying to regain solitude. Am I stupid? Am I allowing myself to be taken advantage of by being my vulnerable, naive, and foolishly innocent self in a possible fuck-up-your-mind-and-heart circumstance? These questions are embedded in my post-dream panic. I calm myself and know that the idea of being "taken advantage of" does not actually exist in my world, as no one can be incriminated except by one's own gavel. If I allow myself to proceed down a path with a very uncertain and unlikely outcome, with unfathomable pain of loss and emptiness, and I still press on, I alone am accountable. I will not condemn the external, that which I have made from deliberated choices and actions from my internal world of possibility. I would then become weak and wade into that cesspool of the ordinary I so despise. I want no part of that. Even if the possible is nothing but a detour from my wretched midlife bullshit.

The rules of transcendence insist that you will not advance even one inch closer to divinity as long as you cling to even one last seductive thread of blame. As smoking is to the lungs, so is resentment to the soul; even one puff of it is bad for you.

— Elizabeth Gilbert, *Eat Pray Love*

> We are taught you must blame your father,
> your sisters, your brothers, the school, the
> teachers … but never blame yourself. It's
> never your fault. But it's always your fault,
> because if you wanted to change, you're the
> one who has got to change.
> —Katherine Hepburn

I am thinking of what it would be like for us to give in to the commanding chemistry that stirs in one another. We had discussed this and how we will keep our tactfulness and just talk and simply be together so neither of us will have to face the shame of betrayal beyond what has already transpired from the strong emotional standpoint. Concealed deeply, I want him to take me with indulgence, without restraint, with the drive of intentional and forceful action. I want him to taste me in the most intimate of places and let him drink in my rapture until he is hard with demand. I want him to be unconfined and lose control and fall deep into me in spirit and deep into me physically until he surrenders within the grace of falling. It is only in the falling that he will discover absolute sanctity. He has become the reality from my fiction, replacing the faceless and nameless prose with perfected poetry.

I believe I am falling passionately in love with him. I can feel it stirring in me, moving in me, gathering extreme momentum and cogent energy. I try not to succumb to it, but it has its grasp on me profoundly, and, fuck, if I give in, my entire life as I know it will change. I'm petrified. I can't ever go back to my old life if I let myself proceed. I relinquish my heart and, with it, everything I am. What have I done? I have already fallen. I am already his.

> Falling in love is very real, but I used to shake
> my head when people talked about soul

mates, poor deluded individuals grasping at some supernatural ideal not intended for mortals but sounded pretty in a poetry book. Then, we met, and everything changed, the cynic has become the converted, the sceptic, an ardent zealot.

—E. A. Bucchianeri, *Brushstrokes of a Gadfly*

## December 2012

I had a dress on one afternoon and met him for coffee and a short drive so we could talk and be in one another's presence. When I got into his car, the amount of sexual chemistry began building instantaneously, drawing us and paralyzing our judgement. We both knew we were in trouble, battling the silent decision to make our way to a safe public place or find seclusion and to let ourselves release into that uncontrollable crave, to let our bodies explore what our souls had already indulged in. It became furiously urgent to find privacy, but there was none to be found, driving farther out and getting more restless and more frustrated with erotic rage. Finally, after what seemed like eternity, we found a retreat from reality, and his car came to an abrupt stop. The only thing I could hear was my own heart, which was beating a thousand miles a minute, yet my breath was calm and controlled. He stared into me with a lion's predatory gaze, and I did not look away, daring him to attack. He immediately pulled me close and kissed me deeply for the first time, and then he touched every part of me, deliberately and slowly, before his hands found their way to my panties. I struggled in a last-minute panic to resist his ferocious pursuit. I was shaking with anticipation and shaking with fault.

He says, "Just five minutes. I want you to let go. Trust me, let go. Just five minutes."

I have guilt, and I am nervous, excited, wet, pulsing, craving. Then guilt again. I cannot stop him, and I don't want him to stop. His mouth and tongue start at my ears and neck, then my breasts, my stomach, my sides, and with his hands lifting my lower back ever so slightly, he starts to go down on me while his eyes lock with mine. He is wild and with purpose. My conscious mind plays with me, back and forth again, rejecting and competing, then, at last, succumbing to the rapturous temptation until I lose to him and his relentless and passionate pursuit. I am completely his, and he takes me until I go limp with ecstasy.

After he drops me off, I sit in silence. Fuck. I gave myself to him. I feel sinful, contrition, and shame. I feel embarrassed. I feel disgrace in my integrity, dishonor in my morality. I am about to burst into tears of utter contempt and self-degrading humiliation, but instead, I burst into tears of relief and deliverance. I feel free. I ... feel ... free. I experience an overwhelming aliveness, an elation, and a warped sense of acceptance that tells me this is okay. I will be okay. I am okay. I sob without holding back until I am rinsed of confusion. Then, I breathe and relax in the wake of this poignant aftermath and warped absolution.

That night, I slept in an undisturbed deepness and peace. I had not done that in a very, very long time.

It is the holiday, and people are on break from work, so I have seen him several days in a row at the gym. After working out, we meet to drive to a nearby café for breakfast and to talk. We laugh with ease and comfort. I look forward to his company, and it is almost painful to leave him. On another night, I meet him, and we drive to a remote place and park. We move to the back, my place of refuge, with sin and divinity all in the same confined place. I love it there. He kisses me all over, and I swell with desire for him. He becomes unleashed. I love hearing him moan in his eagerness for more and more. He persists until I give to him without reluctance, without any outside disturbance, without any inside distress. It is just he and I. I am lost in the way he looks at me. He looks past my body and into my soul, where all is vulnerable, and he captures it and secures it, and I vanish from the outside world and dissolve into his essence. I am his, yet he does not possess me. He has allowed me growth and freedom through him. He asks little of me, but I want to give him all of me. I want to please him in ways that will elicit his once-dying passion and ignite him to life and that will cause a deep craving in him to unceasingly prey on what only I can deliver. He commands me, and I comply not as a subservient, but out of servility to the ardent connection and mastery of heart in its rising power. He is reluctant at times, but I will hold my patience for his ease as well as both of our paths to rightfully unfold. Fate will find us, and we both will have no choice in its dominion, but I dream of what it would be like forever with him.

When I left him, I reflected on this feeling for some time. I remember the younger version of this, yet with a girlish, tender simplicity, stating this revelation when it happened twenty-eight years earlier. I fell deeply in love, as I knew it then, and it was precious and transparent in its gullible, ingenuous existence. No holdbacks; just pure trust. I was enamored in every moment, and I honor having experienced that first time I fell into that place of splendor with my husband. Being in love, I thought, was the nucleus of existence. There was no prior true breath until that moment I let it all in.

You were born together, and together you shall be forevermore. You shall be together when the white wings of death scatter your days. Ay, you shall be together even in the silent memory of God. But let there be spaces in your togetherness and let the winds of the heavens dance between you. Love one another but make not a bond of love: Let it rather be a moving sea between the shores of your souls. Fill each other's cup but drink not from one cup. Give one another of your bread but eat not from the same loaf. Sing and dance together and be joyous, but let each one of you be alone, even as the strings of a lute are alone though they quiver with the same music. Give your hearts, but not into each other's keeping. For only the hand of Life can contain your hearts. And stand together yet not too near together: For the pillars of the temple stand apart, and the oak tree and the cypress grow not in each other's shadow.

—Kahlil Gibran, *The Prophet*

*Journal*
December 2012

At a local coffee house:

The man to my left sits in the leather chair alone. He barely touches the small coffee on the table, his fingers lightly brushing his upper lip. He looks lost in contemplation. He wears no wedding band. His right wrist has a Timex watch on it. It looks old, as the leather band on it is weathered and cracked. His hands have cuts that are in the early stages of healing, but they are beautifully characterized with age, like his watch.

I want to hold them. I want to ask him what he is thinking and what his life is like, what lessons has he learned and if he has regrets and rewards. He looks amazing. The sun is blazing on his face and in his eyes, but he doesn't move away. He sits brushing his lip, staring. I feel him. I feel a sadness, but it is real and authentic, and this man is trustworthy and good. He is beautiful, and he somehow reminds me to honor self-sincerity no matter what the cost. He tells me this by watching and learning through him. I will always remember him. He helps me move forward even if only by a little.

Although Dax and I have touched in an intimate way a few times, we had always resisted sexual intercourse, even though we ached for that ultimate oneness. Now, we must cease all physical parts of the relationship until we can regain virtuous character and figure everything out with soundness of principle, as both of us are hardwired with code and conduct. We must make this right for everyone. We must stay away from enticing allurement until it's right or stay away permanently. As we regress in our physical relationship, we continue writing and texting and talking on the phone as often as we can. I am able to find depth and contentment in his writing and his voice. Please, God, forgive me. Please help my soul climb, and let love always be my teacher.

> Without love we merely exist … with Love, we truly begin to Live.
> —Anonymous

> Each friend represents a world in us. A world not possibly born until they arrive, and it is only by this meeting that a new world is born.
> —Anais Nin

*Journal*
December 2012

Once again, I had zero feeling of anticipation for Christmas this year. Just as several of my family's birthdays came and went with nothing inside of me but a glimpse of outward happiness on their behalf. I have come to a place in life that seems like scouring the bottom, yet I will never let myself fall beneath a certain low—the low that people go when they know/feel nothing at all. They go to destruction of self, sabotaging their own essence, a place called hopelessness.

I will never be there. I am most definitely at my ground level. When can I be nourished enough to ascend? I am sitting here at the bottom, looking up at all my possibility. The invite alone is temporarily quenching, yet I feel like the small seed locked deep in shell, unacquainted of its potential. I want to let it come into me, develop me, become me.

> In all chaos there is a cosmos, in all disorder
> a secret order.
> —Carl Jung

> A seed hidden in the heart of an apple is an
> orchard invisible.
> —Kahlil Gibran

I am not without fear, grasping at slivers of courage at however much I can seize. I am fragile and sensitive on the inside, but I have hardened up on the outside for protection during this vacillating time. I hope to lose that somewhat, as this is not who I am. Nor do I want to carry it with me. I want to come back to my openness with fortitude. I am now closed up but not shut down. Sometimes I am lonely, but I know that it is necessary too. I will feel safe in my armor and yield to the loneliness, let it all come and let it all discipline me, let it re-create me.

I am experiencing more and more painful days. I know those are the ones that shake me up and hold me down and slap my face and say, "Pay the fuck attention here. You are about to embark on a tutorial to carry you onward, so sit up straight or stand up tall and pay attention." I try hard not to react as my human self, with an ego that is pitifully sensitive and is ready for a quick fight-or-flight response, but it is difficult to lose, as even I know that threads into the spiritual scholastic. I am learning more to champion a mature response instead of a moronic reaction, to get out of my own fucking human way.

> Man cannot discover new oceans unless he has the courage to lose sight of the shore.
> —André Gide

I wonder where I will be a year from now. I can guide my directions so it is not passive and demonstrates a desired path of intention, and perhaps the divine will intercede with gracious plans for my undeterred fate. I now feel it is harmonic. I know we have great powers inside. I have witnessed the laws of the universe within my own personal work. Yet I have witnessed what cannot be explained and cannot be overlooked as ambiguous coincidence. I love the complexity, the brilliance of it all. It teases my intellect with expansive obscurity.

> I can control my destiny, but not my fate. Destiny means there are opportunities to turn right or left, but fate is a one-way street. I believe we all have the choice as to whether we fulfill our destiny, but our fate is sealed.
> —Paulo Coelho

I met Dax tonight to talk and to have coffee. It has been awhile since we have seen one another in person, and I was so happy to see him. When I returned to where my Jeep was parked, there was a figure of a man who dashed out from where I had parked.

I said to Dax, "Did you see that? I just saw someone right next to my Jeep, and he ran away."

I waited just a few minutes, as I was intimidated. Just as I was about to exit Dax's car, a car pulled up behind us with its high beams directly in the back window. They were so bright, and the car was so close, it was blinding. I quickly became drenched in terror.

I said, "Is it a gray Mercedes? Can you see the car?"

"It is," he said.

"It's my husband. I am afraid to get out. Please, drive. Please, hurry," I said.

"Why not just talk with him. We are not doing anything wrong?" he said.

"No, no, this doesn't feel right. Drive to your gated community, and we can go inside and be safe. Then you can drive out the other entrance and drop me at the local coffee house. You need to go home, and I need to deal with this." I will have a girlfriend come and get me. Please," I said.

We raced at high speed for at least eight to ten miles to approach his private community, and we got in safely. My husband was on us but was retained at the security gate. Dax continued through to the other side and then proceeded to the coffee house, per my request. He didn't want to leave me, but I insisted. I called my girlfriend, and she came immediately. While I was waiting, I received a call from our local police department about my whereabouts, as my husband had made a huge scene back at the gate. I told them what had happened, and they agreed to meet me back at my parked Jeep, as they were concerned with my safety. When I met them, I proceeded with the truth—that I was with Dax for coffee and at drop-off, I felt uncomfortable and was worried about possible confrontation, so we drove off. The officer said that my husband was highly irrational at the gate and that they were concerned with my safety. As they walked me to my Jeep, they noticed that the air had been let out of my tires, on purpose. This was even more startling. This was a chargeable offense (tampering with a vehicle) according to the police, as well as domesticated harassment and stalking. I was out of my mind with fear and panic and began to tremble uncontrollably. The police helped with getting my tires filled, covered me with a blanket, and said they were going to escort me home and likely needed to arrest my spouse. I was terrified. My children were home. They would become afraid. I needed to get myself together, fast.

As we arrived, my husband was already there and was surprised to find four police cars behind me. They searched his car and confiscated his phone, which had an application for a tracking device that had been installed on my Jeep. Also, in his car were documents of results and pictures of my underwear from a high-tech investigation lab in Dallas, Texas, which revealed negative test conclusions for semen and saliva. The police urged me to pursue a restraining order for my protection. They arrested him and took him away that night, and I was distorted, confused, and very afraid.

When I put the children to bed and tended to their emotions, one question came to me as I pulled the covers snugly around one of my daughters and brushed her hair away from her delicate, teary face.

What would I tell my daughters if one of them were in the same scenario all these years? Years of selflessness to the point of extreme self-denial, significant marital neglect, a severely broken and lonely heart, heavy, abusive spousal disparagement, a suppressed and sacrificed soul—all of it, everything.

What would I tell her to do? Looking down at her with such profound love and an intent to create a bold foundation, grow her with strength and steadfast tenacity alongside happiness and a positive direction toward fulfilment.

My eyes swelled and pooled with emotion. As I desperately fought back these tears from falling, I leaned down and kissed her small, precious face and silently promised her and my other children, *truth*. Then, in a fractional moment came the most firm and conclusive, the most deliberate and dauntless, the most unwavering and intrepid decision I think I have ever made.

# PART 3
## *Falling Down*

It is strange how we describe the
beginning of love as "falling" when
in fact, it is the end that is the fall.
Love raises us up, higher than we ever
dreamed possible. And the higher you
go, the greater the fall when it is over.
—Ranata Suzuki

*My husband was released from* jail late afternoon the following day. I settled our children with a movie, having our oldest at fourteen years old, take care of the younger ones. I drove around before he was released to find my needed determination, courage, and poise to stand up to him with what I must relay.

Divorce.

It will be so difficult, but no more wavering and waiting. No more purgatory. Movement. This is now in forward motion, and I am completely terrified, as if I am walking into a third-world foreign country with heavy ammunition ready to take me down with the slightest wrong turn. I pray, I pray, I pray.

I looked outside earlier this morning, and the sun had not let us down, rising today and giving light, warmth, and visibility for direction. I am reminded that I have the same job to do.

I found him walking from the jail to our home by the time I had enough composure to get to him and address the inevitable. He got in my Jeep, and we remained silent until I pulled up in our driveway. I kept the truck running and turned to him. He looked desperate, aged, and vacant, nothing like the man I had known for twenty-five years. I had to proceed as this acknowledgement was drastically overdue. I looked him straight in the eyes and said, "Although I will always love you, I am no longer passionately in love with you, and I know that we have lost our marriage. This has been several years now of falling away from the us we once knew, and we need to move on by means of divorce."

He said, "No … no … you love me. I am not doing this. We are not doing this. We will get over it. You love me."

I said, "No, honey, we need to move on. You know it, and I know it. It has become toxic, and we are losing ourselves within this decline. As you are now aware—and should have been made aware of as soon as it started—I have been emotionally involved with someone while trying to find myself, and you have been absent in our connection and marriage for years and now have engaged in completely irrational behavior, which is becoming frightening to all of us. Look at us. We have been over for a long time."

We just sat there for a while in silence. My head and heart were filled with almost unendurable empathy, but I wanted some way to find the stamina to make it all better for him somehow. Any hint of close intimacy from my heart would stir false hope and lure him where I was trying to break away, so I didn't know what to do. The suffering of his heart was felt with torment into mine, and the anguish of this failing was titanic. I needed to be alone so I could carry his pain as well as my pain and just cry and ask the universe to heal him and to forgive me, please, forgive me, but first and foremost, please heal him—please.

I drive around for hours in an effort to regain composure and think about how I will proceed with the order of divorce. I have been a housewife for the past twenty years and without work experience, so I know this will be incredibly arduous for me. If my husband truly loved me, he will help me and us in all fairness for the sake of our family, surely. We have two businesses, and I know I could work in one of them. I will need to figure out living conditions that will be of comfort for our children as we transition them as well as for us. Most of all, I need to press forward and never entertain a step backward.

There is such a massive relief in not hiding, lying, and sneaking around. My husband knows everything, and I have profusely apologized for falling into another while I was so desperate for self-movement while also being recklessly vulnerable. I can't take it back, and I have deep remorse for the hurt I have caused him and the corrupt character I allowed in myself. However, I do not regret any of it. I know this sounds contradictory, but I am insistent that it was and is urgent and necessary. While I think of all the things I will need to do for my family, I crave to write and talk with Dax, for him to hold me, give me hope, and tell me everything will be okay. He is not here, though. Has he ever really been here, really? It is crushing pain, and with everything falling apart in all areas, there is no reprieve from the anguishing discomfort that envelops me. On my bad days or rather bad hours, I often get mad at my so-called friends, my family, and Dax for not offering some sort of solace in this time of such a depressing clusterfuck of chaos, and I can't find any avenue of remission. I am not really mad at them, just being pathetic and weak and full of sickening self-pity. There is simply no one out there to lift me. No one to cry to. No one to let go to. I need to find it from only one source that can even attempt to make a difference. Myself.

> The best place to find a helping hand is at the end of your own arm.
> —Swedish Proverb

> Character cannot be developed in ease and quiet. Only through experience of trial and suffering can the soul be strengthened, ambition inspired, and success achieved.
> —Helen Keller

My husband tells me that he will not move out of the house. He said, "This is my house. This is all your fault. You leave." I tell him that I have no money to leave and I want to continue to take care of our children especially now, and he said, "That is not my problem." While I continue to take care of things at home, I sleep with my bedroom door locked as I watch him lurk in what seems like malignant hate for me.

One day, while we were talking about where I could work, my husband told me that it was going to be very tough for me in the "real world."

I said, "I could take on one of our businesses and you take the other, we can make this work for the both of us."

He gets in my face and holds my arm tightly while his other finger comes up to my face and shouts, "You touch my businesses, I will fucking *kill* you." I froze for a moment in a state of shock and disorientation. My eyes fall away from his in a sinking, cowering, and submissive state. In that moment, I see two little faces staring at us from down the hall, and the terror I witnessed on them was horrific. I had to make a game out of this so our youngest little girls would not be in such fear. I pretended to laugh, and I told my husband he was funny with his joke as I smiled at him and gently removed his hand from the clutch he had on my arm. Then I went down the hall to attend to our girls. They looked at me with so much concern and confusion. I found that my hands were shaking, as well as my voice, but picked them both up and said, "Let's go get some ice cream," as I quickly distracted them from the echo of his harrowing comments. For the rest of my day and for many, many days thereafter, I only felt deep, seizing apprehension.

The days turn into months, and as I remain in the house, it becomes even more heavy and dark. I maintain my parental and house responsibilities trying to be a solid mother, but inside, I am in fragments and continue to shatter and break down. My husband has elected to get several online dating/hook-up accounts, and the pictures of pussy that come in rampantly make me utterly confused, as he has bashed me every single day for my extramarital emotional affair and continues to drag me through the mud with shame, disgust, and ignominy. He, on the other hand, has over twenty women sending pictures of their bodies with vulgar promiscuous comments in bold captions. Is this worse than my emotional deep connection with Dax? Is it to get over me? Is it just for sex? Is it to get to me? I pretend to be unaware of this and become more elusive and quieter to avoid any further confrontation. However, the confrontation comes at me no matter what I do or don't do. I am stuck here, and he is now here with me, watching me with the eyes of a hawk and the fang of a viper.

My husband corners me in our once-shared bedroom one late evening and is relentless with his anger and oppression toward me with his unrelenting "tie me to the post and beat me ritual" for my betrayal. I swallow his scorn of verbal and emotional outbursts but shut down while he continues on. I truly am terrified inside. I think about how I want to flee. How can I escape? I formulate an idea of where to run, but I cannot. I feel paralyzed in every facet of myself. What if he snaps and pins me down and forces himself on me? What if he pins me down and wraps his hands around my neck and restrains my breath until I am lifeless? I become farther and farther away from the yelling yet also farther and farther away from myself. After hours of this, I don't feel any more fear, anxiety, or any emotion whatsoever. I am like a statue, nonhuman, void of any feeling at all, but I listen to him and try to find the man I once knew and loved within his darkness and horrendous outrage. I cannot locate him at all. The man in front of me is merciless and cruel, and in my very weakened state, I wish he would beat me physically instead of this type of unseen, unheard, and unproven misconduct. How can he hate this much when he claimed to love me so deeply? I am at least the mother of his children. How can he have this much malice? I begin to believe his words of my sickened, degraded character and how all this truly is my fault and I have ruined our family, our children, and him. He tells me that I am wicked, that my children will know what kind of pathetic person I truly am soon, and that I am toxic to him. He said my mother will also know the "real me" when he talks with her about me. This all weakens me into such an emotional abyss as I contemplate his words as plausible truth. If he is being deliberate in making me wretched in misery, he is currently successful.

> From the deepest desires often come the deadliest hate.
>
> —Socrates

The children are unaware of our informal separation at this point, until one of us can move out. I want them to focus on friends, school, and fun as best they can, although I know they have unfortunately witnessed the tension. I had hoped that there would be a move for one of us at this point, but he still won't allow me any money to leave, and now my grocery and gas allowances are heavily monitored. I have sent out dozens of resumes for possible jobs relating to my past education and work experiences, but being domesticated has caused me to become near obsolete in the work force. I have a four-year Bachelor of Science college degree, but this now is only regarded, inconsequentially, as high school entry level. I did finally secure a job at a clothing store, part time, when the kids are in school and on weekends. I make minimum wage.

My job is in a very nice area about fifty minutes from home, but I drive down a boulevard that has strip joints and convenience markets on every other corner, which reaches my needed interstate access. One night, when I closed the store at 9:30 p.m. on a Saturday, I was driving down that boulevard to get to the highway. I needed to stop for gas in order to make the trip back. When I stopped, my bank card was declined. I called my husband and told him I needed gas money, but he refused to put money in the checking. I kept asking him to please help me or come and get me, but he continued to decline and degrade me. He said, "This is what it's going to be like for you on your own, so get used to it. You wanted this." At this point, it was now 11:00 p.m., and I was just sitting there since I knew I couldn't drive on an empty tank. Several men from the streets walked up, and I became afraid when they approached me. They were bad men, dirty, and had been drinking and were strung out on heavy drugs. They taunted and teased me for some time, but one of them ended up putting five dollars in my tank and said, "Let her go." I thanked them and barely made it home. My husband was peacefully asleep when I arrived at midnight. I cried until dawn.

I meet Dax, and he helps me to find strength. I am drained from the emotional corruption at home. He holds my hand and tells me to be strong and that I am light and love. Often times, he is encouraging to me and momentarily I lose myself in what I pretend to be safety, yet he is further away from me than I want to admit. We had agreed on no physical intimacy, and a few times we regressed in our effort, back and forth, from firm standpoint to momentary lapse in another magical world, but for the most part, we stayed grounded. More than anything, he is preoccupied with his work commitments, and I am desperate for him to love me and protect me, but most of all, I want him to feel and receive all my passion and heart. He will not accept it. We had a lunch one afternoon, and how I wanted him to take me in his arms and hold me and kiss me. Instead, we sat across from one another. I do enjoy listening to his insightful wisdom. He challenges me with my introspection, and I love this. We are both aware of being both mentor and student in each other's lives, and this is incredibly gratifying. While he is in deep focus with his work aspirations and the finality of his endeavors will bring him great success, I am endeared with his anticipation of it all. I also see and feel his struggle with his hold back toward me. There is so much passionate chemistry that is locked down. I am impatient, but he remains profoundly focused. I admire it, and I hate it. This is how it has to be until that moment comes when we are both free—if that ever even plays out in our favor or fate. I hold on.

And he knew that at that moment, they
understood each other perfectly, and when
he told her what he was going to do now she
would not say "be careful" or "don't do it,"
but she would accept this decision because
she would not have expected anything less
of him.

—J. K. Rowling

I continue to sleep with my bedroom door locked and sleep
with a small night light like a child so I can feel less fearful at night.
I know my children are safe and he would never harm them, but
my own safety seems jeopardized. One night, at about 3:00 a.m.,
I am awakened by a sound of a rattling noise. I open my eyes, and
I can see my doorknob moving around, and I become stiffened
with intimidation and dread. I pray to God to please, please make
him stop, but my door starts to slowly open. I shut my eyes and
pretend to sleep as I feel him now hovering over me staring at me,
breathing on me, repeatedly saying, "My wife, my wife, my wife."
I move around a little to pretend to stir awake. He is crying. I don't
know what to do, but I sit up and embrace him and tell him that
it is going to be okay as I tremble in fear. I imagine him taking
my life, but I force myself to comfort him while I pray to God to
save me.

He says, "We need to talk."

I say, "Let's talk tomorrow morning. I need to sleep and so
do you. Please."

He says, "No, we will talk now."

"Please, I say, I promise, after the kids go to school tomorrow,
we will sit and talk." He suddenly switches emotions within an
exhale and becomes angry and starts yelling at me and demeaning
me again and I remain passive and aloof. He slams the door after
he verbally vents. I relock the doorknob but stare at it the rest of
the night, too afraid to shut my eyes.

About a week later, my husband comes up to my bedroom. He says, "I need to tell you something, and it is going to hurt you very deeply, but you need to know. The man you were or still are seeing is using you. He is a master serial cheater and uses vulnerable women to his benefit. He has manipulated you, and I have found out he has done this with many, many women over his lifetime. He uses powerful, divine-like, clever words to lure you, compliment you, until he has you. You are just another trifling amusement. I am sorry, but you needed to know this, and I could not know this information and keep it from you."

For a moment, I sink in despair and dejection. I begin to fall into my husband for comfort and consolation. He takes me in his arms, holds me, and he says, "I am here for you. I am right here." He holds me momentarily, and then my mind thinks of Dax and what I know and believe of him in my heart. I think about my husband and how he has been to me lately, and I abruptly pull away from him. I am dazed and torn in a fucked-up distraction. I tell my husband I need to be alone, and he touches me and says he is right here when I need him. The next day, I go to the basement of our shared home and I am looking for graph paper in his office down there for my son's math class. I am moving files on the shelves behind his desk, and there is a box that I have never seen. I am curious and I peek inside. There are at least eight to ten books on how to manipulate women. There are website addresses with a men's "club" on how to entice women through powerful attraction phrases and bait them into the bedroom. These books have been carefully studied by him, as they had been highlighted/ underlined in specific marked chapters. I begin to tremble and fall to the basement floor to find my breath. I cannot trust anyone right now. Not anyone. Fear and suspicion are growing in me like a deadly plague.

The moment there is suspicion about a person's motives, everything he does becomes tainted.
—Mahatma Gandhi

Within my heart is lurking suspicion, and base fear, and shame and hate; but above all, tyrannous love sits throned, crowned with her graces, silent and in tears.
—William Hazlitt

June 2013

Six months have now gone by since my husband was released from jail that night. He is seeing a girl fairly steadily, and he even takes her back to meet the family. During this time, where he is feeling "lighter," he is less attacking on me. One afternoon, he hands me the papers—serves me. I take them and look down at them and then look up at him. We stare at one another as if in momentary confusion of it all, as if we have been stung by some shocking news that neither one of us knew was coming. We stare and stare deeply into one another, and then I drop a tear, followed by another and yet another. He puts his bags down and takes my face and wipes away the emotion, but they keep coming. He holds me, and we both cry and cannot let go of one another. The pain is piercing, and I hold him to protect him and he holds me to attempt to shield me from it all, but we both know there is nothing but the pain. We just hold and cry … hold and cry. Breaking down in one another's arms. Wanting to console one another, but there is nothing but immense misery, failure, love, as well as relief bleeding from the both of us. After a while, we pull away, and we are so thick with suffering, but we release our embrace, and I watch him leave as he softly whispers from his lips that he loves me. I return by whispering it back, and then I watch him slowly drive out of our driveway. For that brief, fleeting moment was the return of the man I had once loved so passionately.

I sit alone for the rest of the day and memories flood my mind when I walked down the aisle in great anticipation to be his wife. The mere touch of his hand was my world and his kiss was my eternity. We were inseparable, and our wedding was stunning, with such abundant promise of joy. Six years later, our first child was born, followed by three more. I felt as if I had the universe in the palm of my hand, cherishing it gently every perfect minute. I was his wife, and it was such grandeur. I loved him with all that I had inside, outside, and around me.

A wife: it was a declaration of my commitment to him and it stood for something; it stood for everything in the uppermost reverence. I will miss this feeling of belonging, in a "home" that I once was accepted and that I was loved, cherished, and fervently adored. I stare at my house that I will have to leave soon, the house that I made a home for ten years here. I see my children playing on the floor when they were little. I see the smile on my husband's face when I surprised him with his favorite dinner. I see my eyes light up as he hands me flowers after a long day's work for no other reason but that he loves me. I see the way the sun stretches across the family room floor and how we would lie in it and absorb our love within the warmth of its brilliance. I sit at the kitchen table and look into our backyard, and I see the kids running around with laughter. I see my husband playing Frisbee with them, chasing them as they smile in the lightness of life. I see happiness. I do not, in this detailed glimpse of my past, see any of the cold darkness that has shadowed us over the past years. For one brief moment, I digest this most beautiful reflection. I close my eyes and it becomes evanescent.

> Only time will tell as our memories fade into a past that isn't meant to be part of the future. Eventually, we have to find a way to let them go, to move forward and accept what's to come.
>
> —A. M. Willard

I know that often when we are going through difficult times that we can go into a shock mode to offset pain. I am certain I did this when things became bad. Now, I have realized it, and it is difficult to face my consequences and the heaviness of failure to my marriage and keeping this family intact. People tell me this kind of grief never goes away. I feel like I am holding onto a life cord. I am watching it and grasping at it, but it is slipping from my grip. I can't hang on to it; it keeps slipping away. The fall is inevitable, and I have no one and nothing to hold on to anymore. I am terrified. Is it loss? Is it uncertainty? Is it all the remorse? Is it fear? Whatever the reason, I unabashedly sob. Divorce is worse than natural death because death just comes. With divorce, it was possible to revive, but you opt to euthanize it. It is all on you. I am within the cavity of emotional turbulence.

I sob again and again. I feel absent from everyone. I feel removed from existence. My world suddenly seems very tiny and I feel insignificant. I don't want to be a nuisance to anyone, and I certainly don't want to feel sorry for myself. Pity weakens strength so I need to move through this alone and with conviction even if I feel I have nothing left. I want to isolate until I can find my backbone. I did this; I can't complain or recoil. I am afraid. My God, I am so very, very afraid.

> If you build the guts to do something, anything, then you better save enough to face the consequences.
> —Criss Jami

> Fear is the mother of foresight.
> —Thomas Hardy

## September 2013

I am in the shower one morning, and I hear that familiar doorknob rattle as he picks the lock. He comes in again. This time, he tells me to stop locking the door that this is his house and his bedroom and bathroom, and he is coming in no matter what. I tell him to please give me privacy while I shower. He doesn't. When I wrap myself in my towel and proceed to put on my makeup in the mirror and brush my hair, he stares at me. He comes over and tells me I am hot and sexy. I say thank you, but I become tense and rigid. He stands closer to me from behind where his body is right up against mine, pushing me in contact with the sink counter. I remain rigid, and he starts kissing the back of my neck. I don't say anything and continue to try to do my makeup. He pushes harder and pins my body against the sink and removes my towel. I want to grab my towel, but I don't. I let it go. I go limp. I don't want him to get mad. I am glad my body is turned away from him so I don't have to look at him. I look down into the sink drain and wish I could be rinsed away and disappear forever. He holds me down hard while bending me down on the sink and fucks me from behind, and I want to vomit from how repulsed I am that I let him and how repulsed I am of him. I wipe myself and continue to dry my hair and do my makeup as if nothing happened at all.

The trepidation of the falling keeps me up at night with such anxiety. I am well aware of how I must proceed but feel caught up in the web of capture. The energy I now use to protect myself has disabled me somehow. I am barren inside. I am lonely. I am unfulfilled. I seek but find emptiness. I find dead ends, dark alleyways. The only thing I can find is a vastness of insignificance. What have I done? My God, what have I done? I must get out of this, and my husband has delayed our court appearance now three times. I need to get a lawyer to help me and guide me. I need to get out of this noxious environment. I do not know how without being allowed any money, but I cannot resist another day.

Never be afraid to trust an unknown future to
a known God.

—Corrie Ten Boom

When a Gladiator goes into the ring, he does
not prepare to die … He prepares to fight
and conquer.

—Anonymous

November 2013

I decide to go home for Thanksgiving to see my mother and my
brother back in our Midwestern home state. The kids and my
husband planned on skiing, so this was a good time for me to
just try to get away. My lawyer is getting things moving for us,
but since my husband has been illegally withdrawing most of
the funds from our retirement and savings accounts as well as
suddenly spending thousands hiring then firing his attorneys, it
continues to get delayed. My husband is also purchasing enormous amounts of clothes and shoes that he hides and locks in the
trunk of his car. The credit card he has in his name has grown to
its maximum. Our businesses are going to be forced to sell back
from franchise to master company. I will no longer have that option to acquire one. When I arrive at my mothers, I am weary, I
am pale, and I have lost weight I could not afford to lose. I still
go running every day to sweat out the bad and then listen to any
kind of strong motivation for the duration, but I can barely get
to my three-mile minimum over this holiday. We all talked one
evening about what's been going on, and I end up breaking down
in front of them.

"I can't get out. I am trying to work, I hired a lawyer for cheap,
but I can't seem to get out of this."

I am trying to hold back my deeper emotion when my brother
looks at me and says, "When you go back, go find a rental home,

and I will pay for it for as long as you need me to." My mother agrees to pay for the deposit and help with the lawyer. I let my emotions drain as they attempt to console me.

December 2013

I search and search for places large enough for four children and myself, and the expense is crazy. Finally, I find a rental house in the old part of our town; the neighborhood is a little rundown, but it's walking distance to two of our three schools that my children attend. My brother agrees on the price, and I am getting ready to sign for it, as this will go fast if we don't proceed quickly. Then, my mother calls and tells me it's too much and that I really shouldn't burden my brother with this at all, that my husband and I should try to work it out, that this is hard on the kids. I am disoriented and confused.

Just as I hang up the phone, I receive a text that another family is going to sign on the rental. I am pacing rapidly around the house, and I feel myself start to shake with fear, entrapment, and utter defeat. My breathing becomes rapid, in a panicked-like state, and I feel like I will lose consciousness. I stop in the middle of the house, and with everything I have vocally, I shout at the top of my lungs at my God:

"Why? Why, God? Why are you keeping me here? How could you keep me here? Whyyyyyyyyy? I am dying inside, and you have abandoned me! Fuck this! Fuck! Fuck you!

I collapse and weep into what seems like annihilation. I just lay there, for hours, alone. I fall asleep from the exhaustion, until I hear a ding from my phone—a text. My brother messages and says, "No matter what, sign the lease, get out. Do not listen to Mom. Your husband has been talking with her nightly and filling her mind with stories and causing her to feel sorry for him. Get out."

I immediately called the rental agency to check on the house, and luckily, the other family decided to decline. I sent over the deposit and I moved that weekend with a small U-Haul, my clothes, my bed, and my Jeep. I left everything else.

> Had I not created my whole world; I would
> have certainly died in other peoples'.
> —Anais Nin

December 2013

I am moved in and for what seemed like days. I crawl into bed and bury myself under my covers and shut the world out. I do not want to wake up. The children will be spending half their time with me, and I must get ready so they can feel at home here. I try to get up, and I can barely move my body; it is so heavy, as if I have been swallowed up in the cavity of darkness for years. I want to sleep off this exhaustion and find solitude as my savior. I drift in and out. Then thoughts of my father come to me.

My father was a brilliant man. He had many issues with society as a whole, but his philosophical theories were of great perspicacity. However, year after year, he slowly pulled out of life. His existence outside his comfortable dwelling became increasingly only a means to gather his groceries and fetch the mail, or maybe see his ninety-year-old mother for a game of cards. He was genius in intellect, and his listening skills were impeccable. Sitting with him discussing life would have been a treat to the greatest of sages. I was incredibly fortunate. I watched my dad fall into deep depression and uncontrolled OCD. His retraction from the world and his growing isolation became parasitical to his life. Deterioration bred rampant within this isolation and darkness, extinguishing the light of his very own spirit. Dad was only sixty-eight years old when he died.

With my eyes closed, I feel him there, urging me to get up, reminding me how painful and debilitating that was and it didn't have to be that way now with discipline and faith in myself. I feel his gentle hand in mine, and he pulls me up out of bed. I open my eyes, and I am standing for the first time in days. I walk to the window and observe the beautiful blue sky and feel the warmth and brilliance of the sun on my skin and thank my father for coming to me. I go splash cold water on my face, and I walk outside and breathe life into myself. I go get my paint from the garage and proceed to paint the walls in an effort to make the little rental a warm home for my children when they arrive.

January 2014

I am now working two jobs to try to make it. I sold my wedding ring one afternoon when I had no food. The ring was valued at around $4,500, and I was only able to get $250 for it, but that was food money, and it had to be done. I am able to make it appear as if I am fine with groceries by eating minimally while the kids are with their father and stocking up with their favorites when they come home to me. I do not feel sorry for myself; nor will I reveal any sign of outward hardship to anyone, including myself. I feel I am making it, no matter what. I get surges of empowerment within the struggle of survival. My husband is supposed to help us by law in our temporary orders. He will not. I know this divorce is going to get much worse. I also know that, no matter what, he will never comply with whatever agreement he signs, even if it is by state law. I am on my own to provide for our four children. I need to work harder and figure out a way to make it all work out for everyone. I will do this.

I think of Dax every minute of every day. We still meet here and there, and even though I am completely and madly in love with him, he is exactly the same. He has told me he loves me only a few times but tells me that we will be together one day.

Hearing this intoxicates me and elevates me. I ask if he has moved toward separation or divorce, or what his plans are. He tells me to "relax and to trust." He tells me a lot of amazing things that feel like the high of a cocaine rush, but he continues to go home every night to his wife, who I am now guessing must be oblivious to it all. This begins a gnawing at my once-confirmed trust in him. I feel sad for her. I feel a sense of disrespect for him. I feel used, and I feel cheap.

I run earlier every day now, at 5:00 a.m., and go to the gym five days a week for weights and spin classes. I need to be stronger. I went to spin class yesterday, and the instructor said, "Man, this hurts," and I loved hearing it. We push ourselves into physical pain at the gym. One more rep, one more sprint, one more, one more, one more. The next time we push, we are built to start at a higher level, building ourselves for strength and the courage to move through pain so we can not only conquer the quest but prepare in brawn for what will come next. I have this innate persistent pang that there is much more that I will need to endure. I will prepare fiercely.

Money is so fucking tight, but this place is mine. The kids are doing well except the first couple of days after they return from their father's house. They are quiet and appear beaten down. I am fearful he is now attacking them in my place. They do not talk about any of it. They seem threatened if they do speak about it. Surely, he would not hurt them. My God, what if he is hurting them? I will pay very close attention to their emotional well-being, and I will do whatever I need to do for them to be safe, no matter what the cost.

Time is a rush and becomes cyclical as I become the running hamster on a never- ending wheel. I am engrossed in becoming the best financial provider, mother, and housekeeper, the parts of a father that the children have lost, the top employee, everything. I have very few friends, and my extended family is remote. My husband's disdain for me continues to increase, and he takes notes on me and my whereabouts and has also broken into my rental home and stolen prudent information from my desk that were privy to my attorney as well as other things that went missing. I am afraid of him and his obvious pursuit of vengeance. Oddly, I am finding myself amnestic, with a lot of the painful things from the past, as if the memories are suspended in a dense fog in scattered pieces. I suppose one day, I will have to reach in and force these back out and deal with them, but for now, I need to keep them suspended.

I spend my limited alone time in vivid daydreams of a future with Dax and how precious that moment is even if it is mere desire. I get lost in these "castle in the sky" moments of delight that make me giddy and smile at the thought of such perfection. I blush at the thought of him knowing I dream like this in such absurd circumstances. He is a hard and somewhat calloused man on the exterior, and maybe his work is his only focus in life, but I see so much more in him on the inside—or I wanted to believe in more, anyway. I should let go of these eccentric and romantic fairytales, but oh, the magic it bestows on my heart. I see him in reality for only about an hour on the weekend when he is not working, but as time passes rapidly, now well into this 2015 year, there is sluggish movement forward on his part in regard to our relationship. It will be three years of this connection with him come late fall, and I am more in love with him than ever before. He, on the other hand, waxes and wanes from wanting us intensely, which draws me in close to becoming singular and distant with what almost mimics a coward within weak avoidance, but he labels it as "busy with work." The feeling inside of my gut when he becomes remote is tangled and twisted and in my heart like raw crippling torture. I know he was enamored with me at some point, and although he had told me he loves me and wanted to be with me, I know what true love feels like. I need to let go. My God, how can I let this go?

> True love cannot be found where it doesn't exist, nor can it be denied where it does.
> —Torquato Tasso

The biggest coward is a man who awakens a
woman's love with no intention of loving her.
—Bob Marley

As I think deeply in private, I don't want to live a life where the best of moments are put off to the side, on hold, when the time is right. Then it becomes behind us. That is an imposter of experience, of stale value—a waste of precious and limited time. I have always believed in a life where love is the dominant force. When love and the person you are madly in love with are always first and foremost, everything else in life is pure ecstasy, and it all simply flows. I don't want to ever be put on hold. I do not like feeling uncomfortable in this. I also do not like role reversal. I want to bask in femininity. I want to be the princess sought after, desired, pursued, and fought for. I am continuously put aside to wait, and I have remained in eagerness of the slightest possibility. Maybe I am gullible for romantic gestures, vulnerable to the heart, naive, but I am gaining clarity on my discomfort and disappointment. I understand work commitments, but I know what I need in this life and I know what is tolerable, what is expected—not from him but of myself, according to my intended direction. I can't ask for something that he can't give, as I end up within too many moments of this rollercoaster of elation then extreme let down. I do not want to be desperate for love. I just went through this, and I do not want to repeat the pain. I can't be the girl that waits, the girl that hopes, the girl inflamed with passion, but his passion has long extinguished. The girl who says, "I love you" and hears nothing, the girl who wants to connect on the deepest of intimacy and is refused and rejected, the girl who gives all her heart year after year and continues to just wait. I allowed myself to be that girl, but I am not that girl. I stand at the forefront. I must remember that love from within *is* the forefront, like the epiphany I had years ago. I can't be here. I can't operate this way and I know in my soul that I can only live by one true creed. My conviction of truth. Everything beautiful needs nurtured, including Love.

> Love never dies a natural death. It dies because we don't know how to replenish its source. It dies of blindness and errors and betrayals. It dies of illness and wounds: it dies of weariness, of withering's, of tarnishing's.
> —Anais Nin

> Never allow someone to be your priority while allowing yourself to be their option.
> —Mark Twain

November 6, 2015

Today I am nervous, scared, sad. I am prepared, poised, and strong.

I see him walk in, and I can't keep my eyes off of him. He carries his little red folder, and I have mine. I am trembling in emotion but gathered in stamina, our marriage soon to be permanently extinguished by the forms we hold in our clutches. Our signatures by the very hands that clasped together in promise saying, "I do" will now, by the stoke of a pen, sign off on our once revered and trusted union. The moment allows for a one more flashback of the man I loved so deeply. I reminisce at all that was, and I silently thank him in immense gratitude for him and for our time together. I shut my eyes and take a deep breath. I look over at him again, and this time, I only see a stranger. The suspension of the harsh words erupt in stern lucidity as I remember, *What the fuck is wrong with you? What kind of a wife are you? You are toxic. You poison me. Enjoy your self-absorbed world at the expense of others. You are a selfish bitch.*

The stranger sitting across the room has hurt our children by disparaging me brutally, making them feel shame for loving their mother, making them feel sorry for him, telling them I am manipulating them, anything to get them to take his "side," no matter how viciously he tears into their defenseless emotions. There is constant degrading and shaming and telling them that I am wicked and evil, that I am trying to demolish him, that I am trying to put him in jail. Words: they are spoken, and you can't ever take them back. The echoes of their harshness burn in the seared heart forever. Forgiveness is a matter of courage and choice, but forgetting remains futile. The man across the room quit his job three weeks before our divorce so his income would be zero. He will continue to be unemployed for the next eighteen months while boasting his ski time at 138 days that winter, while I struggle to be 100 percent financially responsible for our family. He is inundated with contempt for me. I see only a stranger. I shut my eyes and take a deep breath again. I look to my attorney and I tell him, "Thank you." Then I rise in confidence as the judge walks in and I raise my right hand and say "I do" one more time.

December 2015

Getting away from it all, driving in solitude, looking at the beauty that surrounds the world, I find her. She is still within. A smile stretches across my face, and the numbness dissipates as the anticipation of my freedom, adventure, and purpose are at the helm of the road ahead. I know I only have a short time to let myself open up enough to know I am still here, awake, and feeling. I have merely been covered by tyrannical circumstances, and I am the only one that can lift it. When I gain more resilience and confidence, I will take flight. Right now, though, I feel the vortex of the deepest fall about to take its genesis. I have only prepared for what is next, not what is done. I am in heavy armor, but how strong is my shield?

Late December 2015

I ask Dax to meet me. I have my letter in hand. I am in excruciating pain. I asked him recently if he still loves me, and his reply was, "Relax." I asked him if he still wants me, us? His reply: "Relax." A response of his throughout the years that I used to love and that used to calm me with a meaning that I construed as, "Everything will be fine if you are patient and trust this," but now I understand the word was used to only abandon the question. Regardless of what he feels or doesn't feel, it makes no difference. My heart belongs to him, and it will forever be his. His heart remains timid, indolent, fearful, and uncertain. I know what I need, what I want, and where I am heading. It is time to permanently say goodbye.

> Unless it's mad, passionate, extraordinary love, it's a waste of your time. There are too many mediocre things in life: Love shouldn't be one of them.
> —Anonymous

I watch him pull up and my heart races. I don't want to do this. I want to fall into his arms and feel him forever. I can hardly breathe. I get in his truck, and my eyes are blurred with tears. I look over at him, and through my agonizing torment, I smile at him for all that we had. I pull out my letter with trembling hands and a shattered heart.

My Dearest Dax,

Journey well:

I hoped that with all my heart and soul that this is not the letter you will ever read, as it will be my last. Spiritually, I accept it because it's your journey. Humanly, I am angry, very sad, and deeply hurt, because it was also our journey.

You have given me a moment in time that lifted me up for a short duration under the bright sun and intrigued me with your uniqueness, mystified me with your depth, and transformed my heart to a level I never thought could surpass prior experience. It is an old adage that people come into your life for a reason, a season, or a lifetime. I daydreamed every day to make the rest of your life full of the love and happiness you deserve and I desperately wanted to give it to you for the time we had left on this beautiful planet. I trusted it, because I trust love. You will not be there. You were only there for a season and maybe even for a reason, ones I must accept because of your choices, priorities, or a path that doesn't include me.

You know that there is a spiritual connection between us that is a once-in-a-lifetime encounter. We are both blessed to have had the moment, the experience, the lesson, the love, the knowing. I will treasure it always. I must be accepting of anyone's personal journey because I want to honor individuality and the highest good for that souls' purpose. I honor you and will love you endlessly.

I have always believed that you were my soulmate—the one. It will be difficult to adopt an acceptance that you are not. We were simply connected for a while, and I will recognize it with immense gratitude, but true soulmates come together and are eternal. Soulmates are never an option and certainly never rejected.

In my human realm and perhaps just my ego, I am so deeply hurt and angry with you for not accepting us and fighting for us. It will take me a long time of grieving and trying to make sense of it all, but I will let you go from my life. As mentioned, so many times, being in your arms was "safe," and it felt as close to home as I could ever describe. Maybe ineffable. I gave all my heart to you willingly because I wanted no regrets within myself or for our chance together. Every time I had a moment with you, it was beautiful, and I was empty leaving you or being without you. You, however, became withdrawn and ambiguous in direction and eventually seemed to want to get on with your day quickly after having our hour on Saturdays. I know I turned a blind eye to this for a while as it was very hard for me to understand as I felt your soul and our passion in sublime unity, and I was convinced I was never wrong in my heart. Perhaps I was in my own realm and perception of love, one I created out of strong desire for a charming and magical fairytale that was without a doubt exquisite but proved illusory. I just don't know the answer to that or if I ever will have an answer.

The anger and sadness I feel is not because I blame you for hurting me (I am responsible for all my emotions), but because you denied your soul from love, you denied us and our opportunity; you rejected our journey. You claim to be a loyal man, yet your loyalty is tainted. You want to be in the light and live honorable, but you don't stand in your truth or let others, you claim to love, know your truth, thus demeaning love altogether. You always talk about standing on the stage and giving it your all and if you fail then you will fail hard on the biggest stage so everyone will see it, that you would not hide. I loved this boldness in you, and it roused such respect from me, and I fell in love with your character because you were daring and unafraid and stood against ordinary. You are a lion in the work world. You have stamina and endurance and you will not give up. This moved me in more ways than you will ever know. However, in the heart, you are a coward. You hide and can't express and won't receive because you fail to surrender to the force of love, yet it is within that falling completely that can allow loves strength to rise to the summit of the boldest of forces ever experienced. This angers me because you are so much more in your soul. I see it in you, and I felt it from you waiting for liberation. You let it fall away.

This makes you complacent, common, and you "settled," which makes you fraudulent in your proclamations and in love. *Love*—the most important force in existence. Forgive my words. I do not mean them to hurt you or anger you. I want to express what is inside, especially to you—the man I love most in the world.

I will never stop loving you. You have a part of me that is exclusively yours, that was always yours before you even saw me that day and will be yours until the end of our existence.

Journey well, my love.

I love you. I love you. I love you.

Jade

Ever has it been that love knows not its own depth until the hour of separation.
—Kahlil Gibran

# PART 4

## Rising Up

It didn't matter that she fell apart, it
was how she put herself back together.
—Atticus

*I was shocked and frightened,* surprised, yet expecting, running from it, then turning around to face it. Everything then nothing, elated and safe, then threatened and lost, but adamant in forcing the stinging present moment. Standing in its face and saying, "Let's do this—all of this." Frailty then stamina, confusion then clarity, unabashedly weeping then consoled by the strength of my own soul, desperately wanting the hold of him around me to feel his vehemence, compassion, and love, then surrendering to the emptiness invading me and the paramount hurt of so much for so long. The inside screams for someone to help me, hold me, and keep me safe and protected, like I am some lost child suffering from terror and panic. I am trembling even in the corners of my essence that I thought were untouchable. Yet have now been exposed to the blunt, piercing reality that is blade to my delicate heart. I look up from the temporary loss of orientation, yet somehow, someway, I was prepared. There was something there that came through for me. With a step back and my head not bowed in the defeat of despair, I fought with resilience of spirit and the brawn of the soul. I whisper to my deepest self, I did not know I was ready, but you knew, you taught me, and you carried me through.

I journey to the depth of myself, inclusive of the pain and the fear that unrelentingly haunts, but that is inevitable and necessary. I will stand as the observer once again as I allow the pain and fear to pass through now without guard. It can't penetrate my open soul. There is nowhere for it to inhabit so it becomes ephemeral while transforming venom to vapor. No matter how intense the suffering, when we allow it to make its way through, it can no longer thrive because it is the resistance of it that causes it to be a charged reactive. Condemnation of fear only enhances its control. Closing down, hiding, turning your back, and shoving it under the rug are all resistance measures that create a master prison of true self. Being hurt is a movement, not a confinement. Openness in spite of misery is the price I am willing to pay for ultimate restoration of self. Bitterness is replaced with tranquility. This is an acceptance of will and is the right of passage to an irrevocable and earned re-creation. Newfound strength in its conditioning with an unconscious proficiency becomes habit for movement and growth. Bless the darkness; light will prevail.

January 2016

> Every night for the next ten months, I cry of inexorable heartache. The pain is critical. But every morning, without fail, I give thanks for a brand-new day of possibility and drive myself vigorously into my trusted independence and my now unblocked and paved way of self-expansion. Head up and eyes forward. I have secured a new position in the construction industry, selling roll-off services to new construction projects. I can now focus on one career for ten hours a day instead of three inconsequential jobs that left me undeveloped and vastly underpaid. I will do everything to make it great for my family.

> Pain into the heart opens the paralysis of our lives.
> —Anonymous

My former husband has and will not pay his legal obligation to me and the children and for the next three years, I am in and out of court trying to collect his monetary support. Even with all the extensions granted to him, he refuses to get a job that is within his high skill level and opts to barely work or work at entry-level jobs. With our son in an out of state college, I have no choice but to work longer and harder in my career. The only thing court did to him was pressure him and threaten to put him in jail if he was going to be noncompliant. This provoked his anger even more, and he used it gravely against me by harshly attacking our innocent children while in his care with his incessant emotional and verbal misconduct and severe disparagement (which all psychologists and legal authority have labeled as abuse). I could not and would not allow this. I had no choice but to fight for full custody of our youngest three girls, which I was awarded immediately by the judge. The girls all were in trauma therapy for the next four years. I never went back to court for the money he was obligated to pay me and our family even though this will cause severe financial detriment to me but will keep him from hurting our children from his unyielding behavior. I will forgive my former husband for hurting me. I will never forgive him for the harm and trauma he inflicted on our children. Not ever.

> There are wounds that never show on the body that are deeper and more hurtful than anything that bleeds.
> —Laurell K. Hamilton

I know that one day, my children will want to know about me falling in love with someone while I was still married. I cannot make excuses and will not formulate a story or construct any lies to keep myself in the hierarchy of respect that they used to have for me. I will tell them face to face. I will address this without rationalization or justification of all the reasons why I allowed that to happen when I had promised to be a faithful, good wife. I will never be dishonest again. I hurt my husband, and his perception of me will always be laden with abhorrence, and this will wear on me deeply, but I must and will accept it. My divorce was inevitable, and my falling into another was *not* the cause of my marriage failure. I will never admit to that, for that would be a lie. However, it was an imperative catalyst. One day, when they are old enough, I will make sure they know my truth. I will neither ask nor beg for their forgiveness. I just want them to know me, my accountability in all of it, and my exalted heart. I will not cower. We all have flaws. No one is perfect, and we must accept our difficult and painful experiences as life tutorials to climb higher, to be better, and to always let go at some point so that we can continue to go beyond the suffering, beyond guilt, beyond destruction, beyond the confines of limitation that we ourselves hold constraint. This is life—everyday challenges, everyday choices. But now, I decide my self-worth, my self-esteem, my confidence. No one else on the planet can ever rob me of that even if they think I am undeserving. Even if the four people I love most in the world should turn away from me. They deserve truth, and no matter what, I will not shrink in order for them to accept me. The only thing I know I can do now is forgive myself, and what my loved ones decide to do with how they perceive and process my choices is ultimately up to them. I can only offer transparency. After all, being in the raw feels alive and this love and veracity begets the freedom I long to soar in. I accept this; I am this.

> We all make mistakes, don't we? But if you can't forgive yourself, you'll always be in exile in your own life.
>                                        —Curtis Sittenfeld

## Forgiveness of Self

I have always been fragile in emotional sensitivity. I struggled with allowing suffering to overtake more of me than is healthy. As I would allow to feel to a depth where perhaps few go, my goal was to be absolute and not partial. However, I found that by allowing empathetic connections as well as personal anguish to go too deep, issues became incredibly painful, to a debilitating shortcoming. I began to exercise various levels of discipline within an emotional balance—in other words, the "take-in" would be experienced with sincere compassion—but not to allow myself ongoing suffering into depletion, or worse, self-destruction. I created an allowance of the emotions with a system to feel it to a depth that is viable and acceptable, validate the emotions, and then let it go. This has had a tremendous impact on the training of my mind to facilitate my emotions for stronger avenues. I kept telling myself over and over that I am the master of my body and I am the master of my mind in every and all circumstances that would arise as best as I could. This has culminated an irrefutable self-mandate to be tough in focus and durable both physically and mentally. I will instruct my mind and body to execute all my intentions from the core of my calling. This includes my intention for self-forgiveness. Forgiveness is crucial to move into a dominion of self-acceptance, where peace is attainable and happiness is inevitable.

> We need to stand guard at the door of own minds.
>
> —Jim Rohn

> If we don't discipline our fears and control our focus, the world will gladly do it for us. It's your choice what to focus on.
>
> —Tony Robbins

While I am beginning to heal myself, I realize that I was wrong about my urgency and demand to resurface. As I look back on everything during my midlife arena of chaos and change, everything I said, everything driven through the push and pull, all fantasies, all questionable morale, all fears, all dreams, were expressed to match desires, to set forth intentions from those desires in an effort to match the movement toward self-evolution within the lessons that transpired. I didn't want to resurface. I wanted to completely re-create.

My mother used to tell me as a little girl, "Be careful what you wish for because you will probably get it." This is from the world's best-known collection of morality tales, Aesop's Fables (circa 260 BC). I always was afraid of this until I understood that this is a powerful source, not a fearful warning. Be careful? No, be specific. I will be tenacious and guide my intentions methodically.

I think about my past fantasies and how they were rooted in a much deeper need than mere midlife lethargy and rebellion. Morality is in constant construction, and just when you thought you have built a mansion, you discover your foundation was amiss. Mine was not solid and can only be constructed in stability through the lessons of experience. Masters are not titled in merit and wisdom without years of practice in trial and error.

> Your pain is going to be a part of your pride,
> a part of your product.
> —Anonymous

> Mastery is in increments, not leaps.
> —Angelica Jayne Taggart

Infidelity, Affairs, and Cheating

These are disgusting words of such degrading low morale. I always looked at the "cheater" as total scum (and yes, I judged when

I was young and ignorant with inexperience). I could never see myself ever considering crossing that line because I had so much instilled into proper ethics. I revered character, and I was proud of the woman I was, yet I was only an inept girl. I never even had a one-night stand as a young, rebellious, and wild high school teenager. I never once entertained the thought when I was an invincible, short, sexy dress–wearing tease in college. The thought of stepping out in a marriage was almost "arrogantly" below me and beyond my proclaimed soundness (like I was some holy saint without defect or flaw). I am not saying it's okay, and I'm definitely not excusing it. However, I will not ceaselessly degrade myself for actions that brought me back up for air when I was drowning in the abyss of catatonic and remote despondency. Could I have chosen something else as a life vest? When I look back on it all, I had tried and failed numerous avenues. We are hardwired to have survival instincts so profound that we will do almost anything when we are gasping for breath, even if it costs us our dignity. We all have a breaking point, and most assuredly, I had mine. I also know that as I was subconsciously breaking myself down, I needed to lose myself completely. The physical element was the only way for me to completely sink my morality so I could re-create myself. I did not know this then, but this was exigent for my direction. There is hidden fortune in adversity. I am not suggesting that I walk free from wrongdoing, but I will not continue to walk with my head hung low in irreparable contempt. I wish I would have made better choices, but I didn't, and it's time to move on. At what point do I let it go and forgive myself? I decide; I do. The rest will all fall into place through both created destiny and ultimate fate.

> It is an infantile superstition of the human spirit that virginity would be thought of as a virtue and not the barrier that separates ignorance from knowledge.
>
> —Voltaire

> You can spend minutes, hours, days, weeks
> or even months over-analyzing a situation;
> trying to put the pieces together, justifying
> what could've, would've happened … or you
> can just leave the pieces on the floor and
> move the fuck on.
>
> —Tupac Shakur

I think of Dax every day and know that I always will. My love has not and will not be fleeting. Sometimes I stare at my phone and remember how electric I became just seeing his name come across my little screen as a text from him popped up. I imagine how I would feel should he reach out. I stare at it as if I can tele-pathically make it appear on my phone, while in a momentary, idiotic self-blunder. Then I shake my head and push forward. As I go through this healing time and re-create my principles, I must have foundational perceptions or ideas to build upon. I also am open to changes along the way as post midlife will present even grander possibilities. I only entertain the now and my life ahead with coherent lucidity.

To love from this point on however, I will be open and love freely, regardless of past anguish. To trust in giving all that I have to give and to know that loving in the present moment is truly all I have to offer. I do not want to give love with any expectation that I could be loved the same way or of the same depth, desire, capacity, or that the person owes me in any way because to love with attachments is not truth; it is conditional. Love is the jeweled crown and cannot or should not be descended from its throne. It must remain above and stand alone in its pinnacle of authentic-ity, beauty, and realism. I know that if I love completely with all that I am then I will have fulfilled my hearts only mission. To let go when one no longer is within that circle of the connection is harrowing heartache, but it is not unendurable. It is gallant and uplifting to encourage the flight of another even if you are left behind. This is all part of the earnest heart.

> Relationships are eternal. The separation is another chapter in the relationship. Often, letting go of the old form of the relationship becomes a lesson of pure love much deeper than any would have learned had the couple stayed together.
> —Marianne Williamson

Love versus Infatuation

Love is whole, boundless, respectful, trusting, safe. Love heals, protects, and propels us forward. Love is seeing flawless beauty that is timeless, ageless. Love hears laughter as a symphony and sees a smile as a masterpiece. Love feels touch as impeccable excitement yet a comfort incomparable. Love transcends through the eyes to the soul and can see an eternal paradise. Love that discovers its soulmate is always fate reborn, which gifts it with immortality. Love knows, and because of that, you do too. Although love has many facets from passionate, climactic love to a sophisticated, wise love, I hope to explore always its unending complexity within its absoluteness and to believe always true love supersedes impermanence.

> In the flush of loves light, we dare be brave and suddenly we see that love costs all we are and all we ever will be. Yet it is only love which sets us free.
> —Maya Angelou

Infatuation is a flash in your life. It is a piece of pie that is insanely delicious but is swallowed up in a few quick bites. It is forgotten as rapidly as the abrupt influx of spark it once fooled your mind with. It is a head game, not a heart truth. There is no soul connection at all but can have a strong physical/sexual energy yet un-sustaining once explored. Temptation is at its highest peak, almost irresistible to deny. However, infatuation is quick to find character defects and is imminently self-serving to the ego only. It is the ferocious blare of a great new rock song only to find its repetition vulgar in monotony. It is plain and asleep to true vivacity and in the near end it mimics a succession of comatose sleep walking enough to stave off boredom that masks the loneliness that hides just beneath the surface.

> Infatuation is not quite the same thing as love; it's more like loves shady second cousin who's always borrowing money and can't hold down a job.
> —Elizabeth Gilbert

I had an infatuation with a guy that was extremely sexy with his captivating eyes and with his enticing body language. He was alluring, with just the right words at the most precise time. He had no interest as far as getting to know me. I met him for a coffee a couple of times, and he was prying into what would turn me on the minute I sat down. I wanted a friend to talk to and to get into his truth, but he was about as deep as a pin prick. I was bored so fast but played around in the company for a little longer, just in case I had missed an inlet of his wholeness. It was not there. I was done. A month later, I saw him, and nothing he could do or say could arouse me at all.

Looking back at the beginning of my desperation to "become" more, I had pronounced *multiple* (likely redundantly) times my repulsiveness of stagnation. Boredom was simply slow torturous death. It was the complacency that latched onto me like a corrosive cancer, and I was solely responsible for my remission.

Complete healing needed to come from contentment. The contentment could only be rewarded through the becoming.

## Complacency versus Contentment

Complacency fucking chokes the ever-living breath out of me. Yes, I am a little impatient, but there is life to boldly encompass in a very limited amount of time. Because I am all about the love and the growth within the love, complacent marriage is even worse. This is why the nurturing in marriage or any passionate relationship should stand vanguard with keeping it strong, moving and expanding, and keeping it alive with fervor and spark. I don't understand why, when something deemed most important in most people's lives, gets so taken for granted, allowing complacency to breed rampant in an environment of utter dullness and apathy. Complacency is a flat, inactive, sluggish decline in the core of one's personal progression. It slowly rots at the advancement of self.

> Life requires movement.
>                     —Aristotle

Contentment is comforting and safe and supportive. Contentment breeds expansion of the love that already has a history of grand passion and excitement, thus opening wider dimensions of trust within that relationship and the totality of life. Contentment is patient because it comprehends. Contentment is what I want to feel in any relationship where I give of my heart. If there is not contentment, there would not be any sustenance within my heart. Without contentment, the relationship would collapse from malnourishment and would wither as does anything with malady. The most enlightened and immaculate contentment is self-contentment. It is like coming home. Exalted by gratitude, richness, and purity.

Contentment is the only real wealth.
—Alfred Nobel

While moving into my space on the "outside of the circle" or the perimeter, right as I was about to launch out of domestication, my former husband always accused me of being self-absorbed or selfish (putting it much more polished than he firmly relayed). I was saddened by this demeaning allegation, as that was so far from who I was and still am today. I think so differently than most, but I am only of my deepest sincerity.

Selfishness and Self-Respect

Selfishness

I have fully devoted most of my years to my husband and my children. As written a thousand times (again, probably redundantly), I have no regrets, don't plan on having any regrets, and most assuredly have no resentment at this steadfast, selfless giving and time during those precious moments within my devotion. Now, I have paved the way for a place that I can dedicate action to what is next in my journey. I am not defined by my role as a wife; nor am I defined by my role as a mother. I will not be defined by my career. I do not want a role to encumber me, confine me, or define me. I am more; I am much, much more. Selfish—I don't even know if that word exists anymore in my world. I want to be all that I can so that I can give of everything that I am. If I hold back or cave myself or give myself in fragments before I am fully developed or whole, what good am I to anyone to have just been passive or partial? Who are people to even say shit like "You are selfish"? Better question: Why are they saying it? Really, if it is better for them we stay someplace tucked under a wing to only benefit their needs, wouldn't that be selfish on their part? Fuck that word.

Selfishness is not living your life as you wish. It
is asking others to live their lives as you wish.
—Oscar Wilde

## Self-Respect

This I have utmost esteem for. If you have acquired self-respect, everything seems to fall in natural order. I am richly supplied with confidence when I hold myself in an earned reverence. This is dignity to my soul. The more I empower this within, the more greatness I can serve to others. I am more; therefore, everyone and everything else gets more. I am not being egotistical here. I am being of worth, as we all are and as we all should innately remember. We are all unique and significant and complete. Looking inward and trusting our true inherent self, then sharing this with the world, is not only bold but essential in continuity. By honoring your own gifts, talents, and skills with fortitude is respect for oneself, which, as a whole, is revering your God. I will be scrupulous in feeding the hunger of advancement thus ennobling the perpetuation of self-respect.

The greatest thing in the world is to know
how to belong to oneself.
—Michel de Montaigne

## Regret versus Remorse

### Regret

I am very cautious with this word. For me, it means, "I wish I did or didn't," and it implies a fictitious change in your history that is only concocted from imagination with blatant disregard to the ripple/butterfly effect that no one can possibly foresee from an illusory scenario. Like a stone cast off into the water, each ripple has significance and a ring of worth and congruity. I am sagacious with the choices I make, and I try not to make the important ones without meticulous consideration. However, sometimes in life, you proceed with either impulse or intuitiveness. What transpires, regardless, is the lineage rich in the scholarship of wisdom. Mistakes are pertinent on our human journey. I have been at fault for wasting time pontificating over the alternate outcome and playing out a completely detailed story of events that could've/would've happened. Fuck, man, we don't know what could've happened. How could we? Regret has no relevance; it cannot exist and is a total waste of thought and theory. All we have is the moment, and what we do and the choices we make are ours to avail and weave into the tapestry of life's grand adventure.

> Never look back unless you are planning to go that way.
> —Henry David Thoreau

> Accept everything about yourself- I mean everything. You are you and that is the beginning and the end, no apologies, no regrets.
> —Henry Kissinger

Remorse

Fuck. I have remorse. It is an emotion of deep sadness and guilt from wrongdoing. Some dictionaries will define remorse as regret, and perhaps these words, at one time, were congruent, but today, I do not agree. They are very different words in our modernized language. Happiness and fun are not the same. Joy and enjoy are not the same. Fear and panic are not the same. I have remorse every day for the hurt I have caused someone I love and care for. It is not human nature (for most good natured/normal individuals) to want to illicit intentional pain on anyone. I believe in the goodness of mankind. I believe in heart. It doesn't make me vindictive because I hurt my husband. It makes me shameful, disheartened, and very remorseful. I am a good person who made not-so-good choices in how those choices could affect others. I have to carry the word "remorse" with me for the rest of my life. However, I do believe that goodness will always achieve victory.

> Remorse is the echo of a lost virtue.
> —Edward G. Bulwer-Lytton

> All nature is the rapid efflux of goodness executing and organizing itself. Evil is only a surface phenomenon: the wise person, who sees the profound truth, understands that good is always ultimately triumphant.
> —Ralph Waldo Emerson

I think about this incredible mysterious life and how it all comes together so perfectly if you just pay attention to your truest essence. As a small child, I had already been born and instilled with the exact characteristics that I played out in my life and that I craved in midlife rebellion to bring back. If you veer from truth, truth will find you.

When I was a little girl, I played with dolls. I had a lot of them. I even had two boy dolls that were endowed with a penis. I thought it was magnificent. I played with them for hours on end, day after day after day. I wanted so much to be a mother, as most little girls do, and I knew that, one day, I would have many children of my own. I never had a husband when I played. I was just a mother immersed in the love and nurturing and adoration of a child. I loved it for many years, and then suddenly, I was complete—*motherhood*.

Then, I set out to discover the world riding my stick horse

my mother made me out of an old broom and a large stuffed sock for its head. I rode and rode all over the yards adventuring. Me and my horse, the sun and the wind in my hair. I would often go topless and would frequently be seen with gun holsters at my side and a cowgirl hat. When I outgrew my stick horse, my bike was my horse. I even covered it at night with a blanket in its stall I made in the garage. My horse-bike and I would then venture out on longer excursions of grand adventure, seeking something but not knowing really what. I would just pack a snack or lunch, pretend to saddle up and ride. I would ride fast. I longed for excitement of pretend peril and thrill of renegade escapades and the freedom it ensued on my spirit. I was the world and the world was in me—*unbridled.*

One time, when I was about nine years old, I created a motor-cycle club with another girl. Our bikes became our motorcycles and we were to wear matching ripped up jean jackets and bandanas to hold our hair and we rode our "Harley" bikes all around the town. I thought we were bad ass at age nine. I wanted to be tough. I wanted to be reckless yet brave. I thought I could conquer the evil because I was strong and had more valor than all the other prissy/frilly girls as well as almost every boy, regardless of age. I would also take off on foot to the railroad tracks and sit nearby and contemplate jumping into an empty freight and ride off just to see where I could end up—*wild.*

Also, around the age of nine, I got my first glimpse of a Jeep. I fell in love with this magnificent "freedom" vehicle and made it my goal to have one as soon as I could possibly afford to do so. I imagined the jeep emblem on my steering wheel when I drove my old fifteen-year-old Buick sedan. I would see one parked in a parking lot, and I would walk toward it as if I would be getting into it. I hung pictures of Jeeps in my school lockers and since then in my closet. I bought my Jeep in February 2012 at the age of forty-four, and I will never drive anything but—*boundless.*

When I was ten years old, I rode horses. Real horses, fast

horses. I would saddle up, and we would race the trains at all out top speed. I wanted to be the female version of the Lone Ranger or the beautiful side kick to Tonto (which I would be irresistible in the heart to him, of course). I wanted to be a version of Jesse James (a threat with grit and guts but no killing). I wanted to be a rebel, against the "normal, boring town folk" yet revered and hats off when I rode into that tiny little family town because I saved lives instead of taking them, yet I was bad in a renegade way that others deemed as intimidating, and I liked it that way. I wasn't a part of that town unit yet accepted even though I was a wild, tattooed maverick. This has always been in my blood, through imagination as a child, through my spirit that knows then and knows now that I cannot be kept, I cannot be controlled, I cannot be tamed, cannot remain domesticated. I was born wild and destined to run free. I will not be contained, contained within a self that I am not and attached to any one person in a shackled lock. However, I fervently long for passionate love that fills me up with that immeasurable inner high, surmount to life itself. There is nothing better than this. This is my altruistic highest self—to be free within the absolute of love—*absolute*.

Years went by as an adolescent, and I would roll down my windows in my parents' car to hear the loud engines of cool, fast cars and would feel the uprising of energy from its virile and stealthy pulse of excitement it brought to my senses. I would be in attentive conversations with my teen friends, and a Harley Davidson would rock by, and I tuned out of dialogue instantaneously to watch the ride and feel that same call to the wild within me—freedom, baby. -*Freedom*.

Was my subconscious responsible for the underlying reasons for my "out" in my marriage by inherent genetic disposition to be wild and free? Where do our intentions derive and drive from? Destiny? Fate?

Destiny versus Fate (The Power of Intentions and Focus and the Power of the Divine)

Destiny

When my father was dying in the hospital, a ventilator kept him alive even though we knew he would want to be unplugged from this misery. I was looking down at him, knowing that the very scenario he was experiencing was one he imagined in haunting fear all his life—suffering. Dad talked about suffering a lot. He fixated and focused on this dreadful topic and how it would anguish him in mere thought or, worse, personal experience in his future. I thought back while looking at him lying there, how depressed he was with his mental illnesses but how he had his part in feeding it instead of fighting it. I pleaded with my father when I was ten years old to please come out into the light. He was sitting in his dark bedroom with all the heavy drapes closed up, slumped over in a rocking chair, in total, utter despair and defeat.

"Daddy, please, please just get up and come outside? The sun is out. The sky is a beautiful blue. Just come outside and sit on the swing with me. Please, Daddy."

He replied, "Just leave me. Life is hopeless. I just want to die. Please just leave me alone to die."

This was devastating to me in such excruciating sadness to say the least, but it also angered me. I liked men to be strong and be attackers of fear. Slayers of sadness. It made me feel safe knowing I would be protected under the virility of courage should monsters lurk or melancholy linger, but Dad was too overcome within his internal demons. Instead, I fought. I fought for me and I fought for him. Fuck, I fought for him for such a long time after that but realized later he could only heal from his own intentions, not mine or anyone else's. I then solely focused and fought for my personal intentions and decided that the only way to create a life of power, happiness, resilience, and fulfilment was to have indomitable spirit and construct your destiny through the power of focus and intentions and dreams pushed through organized thought. I used this when I was very sick, in and out of the hospital in my early twenties with an undiagnosed and life-threatening illness that lasted many years. At first, I was consumed with anxiety and fear of this illness, its undetermined cause and diagnoses, and the possibility of dying from it. I went to the ocean for some time while I was incredibly weak, and I stared at its powerful movement and finally just asked myself, "Do you want to live, or do you want to die? Do you want to sit in a dark room awaiting death?" From that moment on, I never entertained the thought of myself as being sick or dying, not ever again. I wanted to *live*. I began to only thank my body in genuine gratitude for its health, stamina, and purpose. I healed myself within a year to complete recovery. I think back on this most recent midlife transition, and I asked if I was creating my path several times (probably redundantly again). Without any more doubt, my desires were absolutely set forth with full intention. Destiny is defined as the hidden power *believed* to control what will happen in the future. Belief is within our control in our human capacity as we create and act to fulfil our inclinations and exercise choice. Destiny is crafted.

> Every man is a doorway through which the infinite passes into the finite. Through which God becomes man, through which universal becomes individual.
>
> —Emerson

Fate

Fate is defined as the development of events *beyond* a person's control, regarded as or determined by a supernatural power. I have mentioned the word "beyond" several times in this writing, mostly from my objections to any form of coincidence and to the grandiosity of the mystical in regards to the people that come into your lives with such profound purpose as well as omnipotent love that is impossible to deny. I want to embrace what is beyond, yet it is only beyond our human brain to comprehend, not our soul. We have a part in our beautiful human endeavors in which we should be exceedingly grateful, but the infinite within our own entity is within this collaboration; therefore, we are our own masters of fate. We are led beyond from our deepest essence of spirit, our soul, and our truth, unified with and of the divine. Fate is sealed.

Fate will find a way.

—Virgil

## Marriage and Divorce

### Divorce

I truly believe that divorce doesn't have to have such a connotation of failure. This is from society, and it is engrained in our minds that it is horrible and wrong. "The broken family." Fuck this. Broken? I look at how, when we are eighteen to twenty years old, we are so ready to leave the nest, not because we don't love our family but because it's simply time to go. We are ready to move onward. Then we are educated in college and married soon after. Then we have children, and it's beautiful and functional, but then it often happens again—that feeling of "it's time to go." It's not that the family is broken but rather an end to the chapter in the couple-hood. The book is still unfolding. Your story, your life, and your family will always remain intact. I wonder what it would be like if we could all understand this idea, that this could have a different essence and that it's *okay* to move onward. We thank one another for the enhancement and the lessons and the shared journey together and what we made from it and we leave not with animosity but with gratitude and everlasting friendship while also allegiant with your agreed legal obligations to the family. Yes, there is difficult heartache and grief, as with anything that is at its end, but we would move through that with honor and direction. If only we could accept this as a possibility at the beginning of marriage, and instead of us all committing to "death do us part," we could commit to the chapter or chapters we happily unite and then we honorably detach and respect that person's exit off each other's highway of a once-shared road. Easy said, hard to route, but it is possible.

I think about how silly it is when I stand far back. We don't get a therapist or lawyer to help us break away from our family when young and off to college or careers. Our parents are not fucked up when we leave the nest. We don't call it all kinds of names and shame it. Why? Because we *made* the detachment acceptable. Most experiences are transitory. Life itself is relatively short. Transitory experiences from one to the next, from one relationship to another and yet another but all intrinsically connected, intertwining journeys. But along the highway of your life, there are many exits. Some people on your journey stay longer. Some depart on the first exit ramp. Then you will be riding along your highway with heavy traffic, and other times, it's that long, lonesome road. Sometimes, the view is stunning, and other times, you look at boring shit. There are on-ramps, off-ramps, towns, cities, mountains, oceans—all of it, all encompassing. Drive forward. Divorce is never a dead end; it's simply an off-ramp for one passenger from a well-traveled and memorable journey. Amen, baby.

> Some people believe holding on and hanging in are signs of great strength. However, there are times when it takes much more strength to know when to let go and then do it.
> —Ann Landers

## Marriage

I loved being married. I loved being addressed as "my wife." I loved having a husband that loved me, protected me, adored me. Marriage is beautiful and sacred when it is at the place of respect and trust and of love. It's where it should be. If it is not, you should not. I no longer deserved being in something I could no longer hold as a piety of love. I failed marriage in longevity, but I am very blessed to have had the beauty of it for the time we did. In my mind, I had a successful marriage for twenty years. I am proud of that. I do not curse at marriage because mine ended.

Marriage remains admired by me and always will. I will not scorn, and I will never say, "Never again." That would close me down, something I promised never to do. I was lucky. I am lucky. I think of marriage and my consideration moving forward.

When we are little girls, we are touched by the romance of Disney-like fairytales that are engrained in our heads and hearts from the moment we watched Snow White awaken into true life. That one magical day we get to stand and peer into the eyes of the one we will call husband or wife beautifully falling into place, at just the right time. Love is innocent yet bold and sweeps young girls off their feet, happily accepting that honor the moment we firmly declare, "We know," and we do "know." Yet, with time, we change. We grow and evolve and sometimes in our human expansion; our paths carry us on different journeys. With that most precious and monumental time some refer to as midlife, a shift happens inside many of us, a shift with an overpowering calling to allow that change to direct us, even though it is filled with an unknowing and uncertainty that we somehow, instinctively trust with *everything* in our essence. People change, and divorce sometimes happens. While divorce is filled with fear and difficulty, disdain, and often bitterness, sometimes, we tend to blame love for the failure. For a while, we are convinced that we will *never* love again, *never* be connected again, and absolutely *never* marry again. For a while, we seem callous and closed, but in the near backdrop, that calling nudges us further into that personal evolution and gifts that we thought were to never be seen, open our hearts to even grander purpose and a surprising capacity to love even deeper. Wisdom, absent in our youth, builds a richer confidence about who we are, and the understanding of love goes beyond the innocent and bold. We do not seek love; love seeks us, and it is within this shift in life, in the evolution of our essence, in the wisdom gained, and the letting go of what was: we allow a freedom to rinse our fears, and courage stands anew. Suddenly, you comprehend that instinctive trust, that calling, that individual fate that falls deliberately and flawlessly in your lap and the risk of loving again, you thought would be intolerable, becomes something that is irresistible because love is never wrong nor unsure; it just is, and it finds us at just the right time.

> Have enough courage to trust love one more
> time and always one more time.
> —Maya Angelou

From an excerpt from "The Gift of the Sea," by Anne Morrow Lindberg:

> When you love someone, you do not love them all
> the time in exactly the same way, from moment
> to moment. It is an impossibility. It is even a lie
> to pretend to. And yet this is what most of us de-
> mand. We have so little faith in the ebb and flow
> of life, of love and of relationships. We leap at the
> flow of the tide and resist in terror its ebb. We are
> afraid it will never return. We insist on perma-
> nency, on duration, on continuity; when the only
> continuity possible in life, as in love, is in growth,
> in fluidity, in freedom, in the sense that dancers

are free, but partners in the same pattern. The
only real security is in not owning or possessing,
not in demanding or expecting, not in hoping,
even. Security in a relationship lies neither in
looking back to what was in nostalgia, nor forward
in what might be in dread OR IN anticipation but
living in the present relationship and accepting it
as it is, now. Relationships must be like islands,
one must accept them for what they are here and
now, within their limits- islands, surrounded and
interrupted by the sea and continually visited and
abandoned by the tides.

Love goes beyond the innocence and bold; it becomes wise.
The revelation of this wisdom opens us to a valor that will not
keep us callous to scorn or regret but opens us to the immersion
of all that you can give, fearlessly. Accepting risk that is irresistible
because you *trust* the heart. Allowing marriage anew raises this
honor again and allows for the grand reverence for the one we will
call husband or wife; and again, we firmly declare, "We know,"
and we do "know."

Love is never unsure ... It just is. Now and Evermore.

Loyalty versus Responsibility (Commitment versus Obligation)

In my younger years, I know I adopted the meaning of loyalty as
simply faithful to someone or something, undeterred. It is a very
regal and ethical word, absorbed in pure goodness and rightness.
I would have pronounced that, I failed in this department when
it came to long-term marriage, but I am proud of the years that I
was loyal. However, now that I have experienced both sides of this
within my character, I realize the word isn't supposed to allow nor
excuse flaw. I was loyal, then, I wasn't? No. I wasn't loyal to my

marriage, period. I was not committed. Loyalty and commitment run synonymous, as do obligation and responsibility. I am finding that most people are altering the definition of its authenticity as well as confusing it with the word responsibility or obligation. Dax always used to tell me that he was a loyal man to his wife. No, he was not loyal to his wife. He obviously had a relationship outside his commitment with me as I did with him. This is *not* loyalty. He is, however, responsible in upholding his financial obligations to his wife and family, which I greatly respect. It is my belief that loyalty is a word that only exists in dogs and loyalty in relationships is only in aspirations. I am not saying it doesn't exist in some relationships, but I believe it is very rare and has become antiquated in our society.

> Loyalty isn't grey. Its black and white, Your either loyal completely or not loyal at all.
> —Sharnay

> Most people do not really want freedom, because freedom involves responsibility, and most people are frightened by responsibility.
> —Sigmund Freud

Trust versus Truth

Trust is transitory with most of the people I have had relationships with during all my past experiences in this lifetime. In spite of that, I do trust a handful people, and these few are extraordinary individuals. I realize that while there are only this exceptional few, those are the only people who have loved and accepted me with no attachment and no expectations. They love me completely, no matter what I have done or not done. I am grateful for them in my life, and I will always be there for them. However, I believe the emphasis of trust is not really trusting in others but the trust you have of yourself as well as being that pillar of trust for everyone who comes into your life. I have no control over anyone else but myself, and I expect only greatness.

> Self-trust is the first secret to success.
> —Ralph Waldo Emerson

   Truth is from your soul. It is your deepest essence connected with divinity. It is all knowing, altruistic, and whole. It is the calling, the power, the will, the way. It is honest and it is love. Truth drives you, pushes you, pulls you, is you. Truth is your birth and your journey, and it is your inevitable death. It is all-encompassing. Truth is perfected sanctity. This truth in soul has my unfaltering human trust. Something I could have only understood through letting go.

> There is in the end no remedy but truth. It is
> the one course that cannot be evil.
> —Ellis Peters

Lying

I lied my ass off for several months during both my storm of the chaotic cyclone and the revelation of heart and beauty. Lying became ridiculously easy, but it always felt disgusting. It bred into a strong habit, a habit that multiplied like infectious bacteria in a warm three-day-old open, dirty flesh wound, thus weakening my character to one that felt revoltingly diseased. I fell privy to the aphrodisiac of heart, which diverted/blinded my attention to demeanor within this inhabitant of misconduct, but lying regeared my entire engine. I needed not only to assume what this eroding of character would do to my entire personal code but to be an active participant with the grueling lesson and rise up from it. I will stand in the hardship of accountability, fortify my integrity, and never again take the easy way into weakness and degraded self-caliber by allowing a worthless bad habit to invade my posture. Never again.

A lie has speed, but truth has endurance.
—Edgar Mohn

This is the end of this chapter in my life. I was asked, "Do you think you did the right thing? Do you think you made the right choices?" That is an answer that could have many complexities, but wrong or right, it really just is, and I am just me. I have the macrocosm within my soul and the eternity of my heart instilled and intact for my ongoing discovery of the breath of life that presents itself everyday both in daring mystery and in familiar confidence. I am an ongoing seeker, yet I have an uninterrupted peace that was not there before. I am rich with lessons in such a short amount of time that will enable me with the acumen of spirit that dwells as my master and gifts me with the treasure of wisdom outward. All the seeking, the thinking, the contemplation. All the fears that follow from my perpetual "what-if" scenarios. The barrier I had created from the burdens of my own pain and the pain I carry from the hearts of others that I love. The desires I wish for and dream about. The uncertainty, the numbness, the cascade of tears when numbness broke. The guilt of wrongdoing, the high of liberation, the immense sadness, and the tuition I was granted by sinking to ground level. The rungs of my evolutional ladder that I am discovering one step at a time, recognizing when I started to close up and forcing myself to remain open and aware. All these things and more. I am so grateful for such grand lessons to amplify my life. I am enriched with so much insight about struggle and strife and stamina and strength in many ways that were unknown to me before. In all of this, the most potent and altruistic empowerments of the lessons that I give most credit to for rising up came from the letting go. The simplicity of trusting individual truth and the complexity and release of the detachment of my fist-tight control over the uncontrollable. The astonishing belief in the mystical and ever-loving essence in and around me that knows and patiently waited for me to free-fall into the light of my journey and let life itself elevate my soul.

## Domesticated

It was never a matter of not embracing being a housewife and taking care of my husband in a way that he loved and that I loved to give to him as his wife. It was never a matter of not enjoying myself in the rewards of being a mother that I so adored. It was always and only a matter of pursuing and acknowledging individual truth that had been suppressed and stifled by allowing myself to become absorbed within those roles and denying my authenticity at the crux of my existence. I feel released from the impetus of darkness and dismay and revived by the wild and free deep within me, that untamable free spirit that was bridled and corralled but will now and forevermore have a wide-open gateway into the realm of possibility that eagerly invites exploration.

Domesticated:

tame, ordinary, convert—fuck that.

Falling out, falling in, falling down, and rising up—these are just facets of life we cannot ignore or reject because imperative change is born out of chaos, which presents itself in valiant precision throughout our daring, elaborate lives. By accepting these changes, learning, growing from those changes, and determining how we will construct our lives moving forward we continually transform ourselves, which forces us to alter, expand, and evolve through the most present human existence to the depth of our unscathed spiritual essence.

Autonomy—it has long awaited my arrival. I have come.

It matters not how straight the gate
how charged with punishment the scroll
I am the master of my fate
I am the captain of my soul.
                    —William Earnest Henley


The End